Through Mark's Eyes

A Portrait of Jesus
Based on the Gospel of Mark

Puck Purnell

ABINGDON PRESS
Nashville

THROUGH MARK'S EYES
A PORTRAIT OF JESUS BASED ON THE GOSPEL OF MARK

Copyright © 2006 by Erl G. (Puck) Purnell

This book is printed on recycled, acid-free, and elemental-chlorine–free paper.

Library of Congress Cataloging-in-Publication Data

Purnell, Puck, 1946-
   Through Mark's eyes : a portrait of Jesus based on the Gospel of Mark / Puck Purnell.
      p. cm.
   ISBN 0-687-33572-8 (binding: adhesive, pbk. : alk. paper)
   I. Jesus Christ—Biography. 2. Bible. N.T. Mark—Biography. I. Title.

BT301.3.P87 2006
226.3'06—dc22

2006006419

06 07 08 09 10 11 12 13 14 15—10 9 8 7 6 5 4 3 2 1
MANUFACTURED IN THE UNITED STATES OF AMERICA

"Every breath a prayer."

For
Joanne Mary Kimball
and
William H. Armstrong

Contents

Preface ix

Travels of Jesus and the Disciples (Map) xiv

Through Mark's Eyes 1

Study Guide 123

Acknowledgments 143

Preface

THE GOSPEL OF MARK is the codified oral tradition of a Jewish community of Jesus followers who eventually became known as Christians. *Through Mark's Eyes: A Portrait of Jesus Based on the Gospel of Mark* is the unique recapitulation of the Gospel according to Mark—the actual Gospel of Mark given depth and breadth by vivid descriptions that draw the reader or listener more deeply into the Jesus story. In a very real sense, the book illustrates the original Mark's Gospel with word pictures almost as an artist would do.

This work is neither a novel nor a short story, nor is it a new translation. Instead, it is a fresh and invigorating invitation to know Jesus as he might have been. This book is intended to arouse the imagination of readers or listeners so they might breathe the air as they walk the dusty roads of ancient Palestine as a disciple of Jesus Christ.

In *Through Mark's Eyes,* the Jesus story is about life. Even the crucifixion of Jesus is about life through the resurrection. And so, the experience of reading this book is meant to encourage people to consider how Jesus' life continues to teach by word and example the universal message of compassion, forgiveness, justice, and love. This book is written in the hope of engaging people in conversation about the gospel and about who Jesus was and is. Thus,

I hope the book is a catalyst, raising questions and encouraging further study.

Through Mark's Eyes is written for a wide, mainstream audience. It is for people who want to hear Jesus laugh; for those confident in Jesus' divinity and his humanity as well as for the faithful who struggle with Jesus' identity and yearn to see him as one of us; for young people studying the Gospels in Sunday school or a college religion class; for the skeptical yet curious; for adult Bible study groups; for evangelists and teachers introducing Jesus to those who don't know him; for Christians disenchanted with the church and a Western European "blue-eyed" Jesus; for youngsters being read to by their parents at bedtime; and for people of diverse faiths looking for a helpful introduction to the Jesus story.

The challenge of writing this book has been to remain faithful to the gospel story as it is recorded. I have relied on the *New Revised Standard Version* of the Bible as my starting text, and a preponderance of quotations come from this translation. Direct quotes are followed by a dagger: †. Although many descriptive details are added, the intent is to expand upon rather than deviate from the canonical text.

The author of Mark wrote in a straightforward yet compelling style: "And immediately they left their nets and followed him"† (Mark 1:18). Likewise, most of the sentences in this retelling are short and clipped, a style such as a master storyteller might use.

Taking the oral tradition of Mark seriously, *Through Mark's Eyes* is crafted to be read aloud and listened to, perhaps even more than to be read silently. After all, the Gospels are read aloud in churches throughout Christendom every Sunday. Individual words and phrases invite adjusting volume, tone, inflection, or emphasis.

There are also ambient sounds, such as the snapping of fingers or a dog's bark, which accent the story and bring the people and their surroundings to life.

Whether or not to use the vernacular was an open question at the outset. Because this book is written, like Mark's Gospel, for the people of a particular time and place, current commonplace words or phrases such as "OK" are cautiously included.

While the book remains faithful to the original text, it also portrays Jesus as a more "credible human being," to borrow a phrase from Jesus scholar Marcus Borg (*The Heart of Christianity*). Generic characteristics are knit into the text to give Jesus, the Son of Man, texture, grit, and substance.

Often, pictures in Western art portray Jesus as a blue-eyed Western European with long brown hair, a neatly kempt beard, and a clean robe. Jesus must, however, have looked much different. After all, he was a Semitic Palestinian Jew who, in all likelihood, was dark- skinned with dark hair and eyes, which is how many people of the region appear today.

Nevertheless, as in the Gospel itself, there is no explicit description of Jesus in this book, for there is not a single reference in scripture regarding what Jesus looked like. This is consistent with Hebrew tradition, which prohibited images of the Divine. Another obvious implication is that who Jesus was and the example of his life point to what is important and why he is remembered.

My hope is that those hearing or reading *Through Mark's Eyes* will enjoy their time with Jesus and his friends as much as I have enjoyed being the creative scribe for this rendition of the Gospel according to Mark.

Please accept this blessing as you prepare to read *Through Mark's Eyes.*

Preface

Life is short
and we do not have too much time
to gladden the hearts of those who travel
the Way with us.
So, be swift to love,
and make haste to be kind!*

Creator God, grant us your blessing,
through him in whom we live and move and have our being,
and fill us with your peace through the Holy Spirit.
Amen.

*Adapted from the journal of Henri Amiel, December 16, 1868.

Travels of Jesus and the Disciples

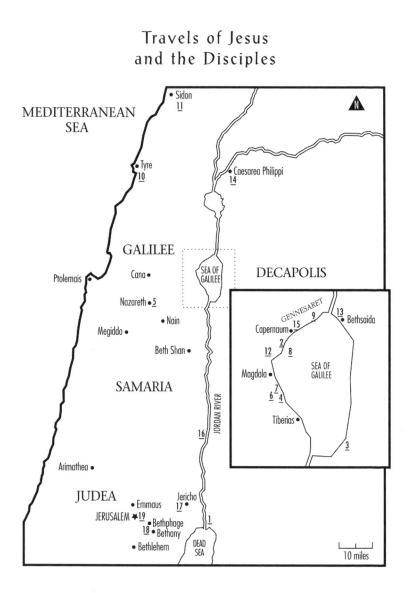

Legend

1. John baptizes Jesus (Chapter 1)
2. Jesus chooses four disciples (Chapter 1)
3. Jesus heals the demoniac Gerasene (Chapter 5)
4. Jesus heals Jarius's daughter (Chapter 5)
5. Jesus in Nazareth (Chapter 6)
6. Jesus sends the Twelve into the countryside (Chapter 6)
7. Jesus feeds the five thousand (Chapter 6)
8. Jesus walks on the Sea of Galilee (Chapter 6)
9. Jesus and the Twelve land at Gennesaret (Chapter 6)
10. Jesus and his followers travel to Tyre (Chapter 7)
11. Jesus and his followers return to Galilee via Sidon and the Decapolis (Chapter 7)
12. Jesus is back in Galilee near Magdala (Chapter 7)
13. Jesus and the Twelve arrive in Bethsaida (Chapter 8)
14. Jesus and the Twelve go to Caesarea Philippi (Chapter 8)
15. Jesus and the Twelve return to Capernaum (Chapter 9)
16. Jesus and his followers travel south in the Jordan River valley (Chapter 10)
17. Jesus heals the blind Bartimaeus at Jericho's gate (Chapter 10)
18. Jesus enters Jerusalem (Chapter 11)
19. Jesus is crucified (Chapter 15)

Chapter 1

"The beginning of the good news of Jesus Christ, the Son of God."†

THE LOUD VOICE echoed. Words vibrated, bouncing off red-brown rocks. Birds jumped into the air and the long river valley woke up. The man took ten steps and cupped huge hands to his hairy mouth. "Are you ready? Prepare. Prepare the Lord's way. Make the path to God straight." He walked another ten big steps and shouted again. "Are you ready? Prepare. Prepare the Lord's way. Make the path to God straight."

A young village girl scampered to her mother and threw her face against the woman's leg, drowning in her loose goat wool robe. The mother stood still in her doorway, arm pressing her daughter close to her. She watched. She listened. The man kept coming, ten long paces at a time. And then, "Are you ready? Prepare. Prepare the Lord's way. Make the path to God straight." The girl squeezed closer into the goat wool. She whimpered even though she had seen the man before, almost every day. Her mother's eyes followed the shouting man. The man walked, stopped, cupped his hands, and called out again.

This man was tall. His chin was far above the woman's covered head. He was big around his chest. Thick, hairy arms stuck out from shoulders draped in a mangy camel pelt with a hole rough cut for the neck and head. A wide leather strap tied at the front hung nearly to the ground and swung when the man walked. A graveyard of bug carcasses stuck to his bushy beard, and live bugs feasted on honey-matted hairs. The man was not concerned about the bugs. "Are you ready? Prepare. Prepare the Lord's way. Make the path to God straight."

Iron voice booming, the man's dusty steps passed the clinging girl and the unafraid woman. Black eyes in sun-dried sockets lit his way. His ten-step cadence and repeated calls echoed. "Are you ready? Prepare. Prepare the Lord's way. Make the path to God straight."

Straight. The desert man walked straight, straight to the Jordan River. His sandaled feet crossed muddy bank stones. He marched right into the water until wet belt ends floated at his waist.

Who knew where they came from! Maybe from as far away as Jericho, Bethphage, Bethany, even Jerusalem. They came and came and came. Children splashed and the stones they threw splooshed. People waited to get a turn. Some only watched.

All day long this John from the desert reached out and wrapped giant hands around the next one. His light-filled black eyes dove into each face, and he demanded, "Do you repent? Do you? Speak your sins. Now, turn, turn around to the one God who is here for anybody who wants new life."

One after another were held in his grip and penetrating gaze. There were women with babies and girls and old men and boys and young men holding shepherd's crooks. They would tell John that they were not pure, that it was so hard and expensive to keep the Law and they couldn't do it but that they wanted God's love. After he heard this, John pushed each person under the stirred-up Jordan water. He held both hands on their shoulders as they wiggled and thrashed, flailing helplessly until nearly drowned. A quick, rough yank suddenly lifted each back into the air where the breath of life, God's breath, filled lungs again and life lighted anew as the water dripped out of their ears and down their faces. Baptize—to overwhelm with water as a sign and seal of repentance and new life—is what John did in the Jordan River.

People thought John was a holy man. Maybe a prophet. Perhaps the Messiah. Or, crazy. Once he told them, "There is another, another man who is even mightier, much more powerful than I. I wouldn't even unlace his sandals. This one is truly a Spirit-filled person. He will bring the fire of Spirit where I only wash you in Jordan River water." John paused. He looked into anxious eyes. Then John said, "He *IS* coming. Get ready."

On a Thursday, in the late afternoon, John looked up to seize one more who had come for baptism. His dark eyes were caught by the equally dark eyes of a man so much like all the others. Olive-brown complexion. Shiny black hair. Wearing a long, dirty, brown wool robe. John's knees weakened. His stomach fluttered, his lungs collapsed, and his suddenly weak arms fell to his sides. A sure knowing shot like a hot arrow through the back of his skull. An arm's length apart, the two men froze in the Jordan River under a blazing sun. The air stood still. No water splashed. Sound vanished.

Flash-like, John's arms wrapped around Jesus from Nazareth. Chest to chest, their two hearts pounded into each other. Then, quicker than Jesus could snatch a breath, John lifted him off his feet and submerged him. The Baptizer held Jesus like he held everybody—longer than long enough—until Jesus thrashed and flailed too. When John yanked Jesus into life again, when water spilled off his wet head and air rushed into his empty lungs, straight out of the blazing yellow sun, a white dove swooped over them. Jesus and John ducked. Jesus' eyes followed the bird back into the fireball sun.

Later, alone in the desert and among the wild animals, Jesus remembered a voice, too, had come with that dove. It was the joy-filled voice of the One who had birthed him in the Jordan's womb-water. That voice was so excited, so pleased with Jesus, "Yes! Yes, you are my Son, my child. You are beautiful, and I am so pleased. I love you! I love you! I love you!" And it was this divine, loving God whom Jesus thought about during forty days of questing when the evil one tempted him and angels cared for him.

John the Baptizer pushed too hard. He was a dangerous Jew. Radical. King Herod snared him, arrested him, and sent him to prison. After that, Jesus went up to Galilee in the north country. He traveled from place to place. Jesus talked about good news, the good news that God was right here, right now. He told those who would listen, "Repent and believe in the good news."†

Good news was radical too. Many people thought Jesus was like the popular John, calling people to repent. Soon crowds were following Jesus.

One midsummer day, Jesus was alone on the northwest shore of the Sea of Galilee. He had friends there. Jesus spied two of them waist deep casting nets in the sea. They were brothers. The short one was Simon and the other Andrew. Jesus picked up a flat stone and waded into the warm water. Hands on his hips, he watched these two pull in their nets. Empty. He skipped the stone.

"Hey," Jesus shouted. "No luck today?"

The young men turned and saw Jesus waving his arms in the air. Andrew put one hand to the side of his mouth and called back, "No fish. No fish today."

Jesus looked to the morning sky. Not a cloud. Gulls squawked as they glided overhead. He scratched the back of his neck and scrunched his shoulders. He splashed his face and wiped the water out of his eyes. He pushed long wet fingers through his oily hair. Then, he called back, "Come here." He waved to them. "Follow me and I will make you fish for people."† And with that Jesus turned, stepped through the gentle surf, and ambled up the rocky beach, robe dripping and feet slipping in slick sandals.

Andrew and Simon, fed up anyway, dragged their nets across the rough beach and heaped them in a pile with the rest of their gear. Jesus watched from ten paces away. "Let's go," he said, and he turned again and started to walk down the beach. Andrew looked at Simon. Simon shrugged and smiled. Andrew smiled too and threw an arm over his brother's shoulder. They walked quickly, laughing, following Jesus.

By the time the barefoot brothers had caught up with Jesus, he had come upon Zebedee's boys, James and John. There they were, just offshore in their father's old black boat. A couple of hired hands were also helping Zebedee and mending nets. They had just returned from a night of fishing.

"James. John," Jesus called. "Come here." He waved his arm two or three times beckoning them. John looked at James. James turned and stared at Jesus. Both men were tired. Time to go in anyway. Without a word, even to their father, they dropped their work and hopped overboard just like that. The two slogged through the water and up the beach to where Simon, Jesus, and

Andrew stood grinning. So then there were five. They walked north toward Capernaum on the shore road. Zebedee, still sitting in his boat, didn't say a thing.

The next night, on Friday, the five went to synagogue. Jesus stood to speak. He talked about the presence of God, that the kingdom of God was near, very near. Jesus was confident. He was clear. His words snapped people awake. His teaching was different from those who usually spoke on Shabbat. Jesus said new things. He made sense in a new way. But his message wasn't what the scribes and rabbis taught. This Jesus reinterpreted the Law. He spoke with a new authority.

Then, suddenly, a wild-faced man leaped up. His hands flew into the air. "Arrrgh. You. Jesus." The man was shouting. "What have you to do with us, Jesus of Nazareth? Have you come to destroy us? I know who you are, the Holy One of God."†

Jesus stood still. He watched the crazed man. He waited. When the screaming stopped, Jesus turned; in three steps he came to the man whose glazed eyes stared right through him. He clasped the man's arms just above the elbows and squeezed. The synagogue was dead quiet except for the man's raspy breathing. Nothing happened for a long time, maybe two minutes. Finally Jesus spoke. His voice was firm and matter-of-fact: "Be silent, and come out of him!"† The man's whole body shook. Jesus held him firmly and was shaking with the quaking man. Without warning a loud scream exploded from the man: "Arrrgh! Arrrgh! ARRRGH!" He went limp. Jesus held him even as the man's weight pulled them both to the floor. Simon and John rushed over. Jesus loosed his grip and drew the man's sweating head onto his chest. Gently, tenderly, Jesus said, "You're all right. You're all right now."

Whispers whipped around the synagogue walls. "What is this?"† "Did you see?" "He teaches with authority and now he's released a demon from this man. How can this be?" "Spirits obey this Jesus? This is incredible." And within one hour whispers turned to talk, to commentary, and to opinion. Jesus' teaching and this exorcism in the synagogue spread around Capernaum and soon throughout Galilee.

Simon spoke first. It was to Jesus. "Let's go. We can go to my house. My wife will make supper." James and John, Andrew and Simon, and the now-becoming-famous Jesus of Nazareth returned to Simon's simple adobe house. There, they found Simon's mother-in-law hot with fever. Simon's wife was terrified. She told how the fever had come quickly and now wouldn't break. She worried because her aunt had died from just such a fever only two years before.

Jesus crossed the front room and went through the open door to the back of the house. An oil lamp flickered. The sickly woman lay on a low, narrow bed. Jesus sat on the wooden edge. The long fingers of his left hand slipped around her limp hand. He touched her face with the back of his hand. He wiped the sweat from her brow.

Simon's mother-in-law awoke. Jesus' eyes smiled into her glassy eyes. "There. There," he said. "You're OK. Come now." And he stood up next to the bed. Without letting go of her hand, Jesus helped the woman sit up. She swung her feet over the side of the bed. Together, they waited. Simon's mother-in-law caught her breath. She steadied herself. "I'm better. I think I'm better," she murmured. "You're OK," Jesus affirmed. "Yes. Yes," she replied. "I'm fine now. Thank you." Just like that she had been healed. Jesus simply said, "You're welcome. You're quite welcome." Later,

Simon's mother-in-law served the lentil soup her daughter had prepared for supper.

That evening, twenty or thirty people arrived at Simon's house. Soon, more people came until you might have thought the whole town was there. People milled about kicking up dust, pushing to get closer to the door, asking where Jesus was. Anybody who was sick or mentally retarded or handicapped or depressed was brought to Simon's door that night.

Jesus listened to each person or to the worried and excited relatives of the ailing one. He said little himself, only occasionally whispering a comforting word. For hours Jesus touched all who came, and they were healed of whatever ailed them. "Thank you, Jesus. Thank you," the last one said before she turned to go home. A cock crowed.

Jesus slept only a few hours. He woke and quietly left the house. He wanted to be alone. He needed time, time to pray and reflect on what was happening and on what to do next. Jesus followed the town road west and then took the narrow path up a hill into an olive grove. He sat against a knurled tree and twirled a stick between his fingers. Crows cawed. The morning's moist breath kissed his face.

All too soon, along came Simon, James, John, and Andrew. "Where have you been?" they wondered aloud. "Everyone's trying to find you." Jesus replied, "Right here where you found me. Never mind." He stood up. He looked into the eyes of his four friends. "Come on. Let's go. We have places to visit. I want to tell anybody who will listen what I understand about our God. God really is with us, even we who are not rich or powerful. I've come to proclaim this good news, and I need you to be with me."

That day Jesus' wandering mission began. He taught about God's unconditional love, cured many people of diseases, and cast demons out of some truly mad people. People far and wide came to think of Jesus as an extraordinary healer.

With each shuffling step, dust puffed around and across a leper's sandals and lower legs. Rain might have made small water balls in the dust—that is, if it had rained. But no clouds had been seen in months. It was the summer season of sun and heat and dust.

Dust puffed up from the feet of others in the crowd too. That dust rose higher though—above the knee and hip, even shoulder high—because those people did not shuffle slowly. They walked quickly. Seamless, dust-colored wool tunics, each woven top to bottom as a single piece with a neck hole cut in the middle, dropped from every shoulder. A rough, braided cord cincture was tied around some waists. Heads hovered just above the dust plateau, all looking and moving in the same direction toward the well, where a pile of people had already gathered around Jesus.

The leper fell behind the crowd's dust cloud, shuffling, shuffling, shuffling. He gripped his stick. Dust mixed with pus and blood-covered arm sores, neck sores, face sores, and places where there were no sores.

Some people wondered, "Who was Jesus?" The leper knew the answer. That's why he tightly clutched his stick and hobbled along the bottom of the rocky embankment and through the rabble encircling Jesus. His "leper license" in oozy blotches repulsed each person he encountered. He stopped in front of Jesus.

The eyes of the one peered into the other's soul. They stood. A dog barked. Then every muscle in the leper relaxed. The stick fell. The leper fell. Nobody moved. Nobody said anything. Nobody would touch him, although everybody wanted him to get out of there. The leper reached through the dust cloud of his collapse and wrapped his sore, infested fingers around Jesus' bare ankles. He held his ankles tightly as he had held the stick, and nobody, not even Jesus, did anything.

After a time, the leper rolled onto his left elbow without letting go of Jesus' ankles. His head lifted slowly from the dust. His red, tear-filled eyes met Jesus' downward gaze. His mouth opened and then closed—his words stuck in dust. He blinked and swallowed and pushed what little spittle he could find across his throat. Finally he croaked, "If you choose, you can make me clean."†

The first tear hit the leper on the cheekbone below his right eye. The second missed him and landed in the dust, making a small ball of saltwater mud. Jesus blinked back more tears. He stretched his right hand down and touched the leper's head. He put his fingers in the leper's grimy hair and held it tight in his fist as he looked at him. Three flies landed on the man's ear.

"I do choose," Jesus said. "Be made clean!"†

Jesus did not let go of the man's hair but held it tightly in his fist. The leper let go of Jesus' ankles, and Jesus kneeled down. He touched the man's face with his left hand, moved his fingers over the sores, and then reached around his neck, gently passing his hand beneath the tunic neck hole and across the bare, infected, scab-covered skin of the leper's back.

Cheek to cheek, Jesus spoke into the leper's ear, "See that you say nothing to anyone; but go, show yourself to the priest, and offer for your cleansing what Moses commanded, as a testimony to them."† He kissed him. The leper moved his head back just a little to look into Jesus' eyes again. He said something quietly to Jesus. Jesus slid his fingers out of the leper's hair and put both his arms around the man. Jesus repeated not to tell anyone. The dog barked again. The people gasped.

Later, when Jesus had gone, when the crowd had gone, when the sun had nearly gone, the leper-man sat alone, his bony back against the well. He was exhausted. He was hungry and thirsty. He was far from home. The man pulled himself up. He lowered the bucket into the well and drew it out. With the setting sun on his face, he glanced at his reflection in the water bucket. Dust, red eyes, and oily hair. Tear tracks across smooth, unblemished cheeks. The man didn't know whether to wash first or drink first.

In the days that followed, this one-time leper could not contain his excitement. Even though Jesus had said not to, he told everybody what Jesus had done, that he had healed his leprosy. Because of this story and others, it became impossible for Jesus to go into the villages. So, he remained in the countryside where people still flocked to him.

Chapter 2

ABOUT A MONTH went by. Jesus and his friends returned to Capernaum. Word spread that he was home again and people began to come. Soon there was quite a crowd. His mud-brick house was neither large nor prominent. It was on a narrow, back street.

A throng of curious folks milled in and around the house. Hardly a sound was made. People strained to hear. Jesus sat inside on a three-legged stool. He talked clearly but not in a loud voice. He spoke of God's abiding love, even for the impure and the brokenhearted. John and James, Andrew and Simon, the women of the house, two scribes from the synagogue, and a few others sat on the floor. Arms and heads and bodies were stuffed in the doorway and three faces poked through the high-cut window along the front of the house. People continued to gather at the crowd's edge. They whispered, "Where is he?" "Have you seen him?" "Has he come out?" "Who has he healed?" And from the back of the crowd there was even a woman who cried out, "Let me through! I need to see him about my child!"

A man, legs paralyzed years earlier by a fall into a deep wadi, was hurriedly carried up the street by his four sons. The old man was confined to a beggar's mat. The sons couldn't get close enough to catch even a glimpse of Jesus. They reversed their direction and cut across to an alley. Two jumped the low wall behind a house.

The other two passed the man halfway over and balanced him on the wall. Then they leaped over. Quickly, with their father bouncing on his pallet, they walked into the rear door of the dwelling adjoining Jesus' house. Nobody was there. They climbed to the open roof, pulling the ladder up behind them. On top, they laid the ladder across the narrow divide between the two houses and dragged their cargo to the other side. Nobody noticed.

In short order, the eldest son yanked up some roofing tiles and started to dig through the mud plaster using a tile as a spade. People in the room underneath looked up when they heard the racket. Dust and bits of rubble began to fall on their heads, and they moved away. Simon jumped to his feet, fists clenched on his hips. He demanded in a booming voice, "What is this? Get back or the ceiling will fall. Look what you have done. Away! Get away!"

The roof-ripping brother ignored Simon's bluster and finished cleaving a big hole in the roof. The room below was full of dust and roof chunks. It was a mess. When the hole was large enough, the sons began tying ropes to their father's mat. Everybody was standing now, except for Jesus. He sat silently and watched as the men lowered their father on his mat down onto the dirt floor. People scattered. The four sons' burly heads immediately filled the hole and watched.

Silence hovered in the late afternoon heat. Dirt-flecked faces turned nervously. The man pulled himself with strong arms to Jesus. With face lowered, he whispered the word "Rabbi." Jesus reached down to the man's bearded chin. With only the slightest upward pressure, he invited the man's eyes to gaze into his own. People shuffled, and the calico house cat sprang to the table top.

After ten seconds, maybe twenty, the man raised cracked brown hands and held them, palms together, between his face and Jesus' face. His mouth was shut.

When Jesus spoke, he said this: "Man, you have great faith and strength. Nothing else is required. God loves you, and what sins you have committed are forgiven. You are a child again, God's own child. Be well."

Gasps escaped the scribes' throats. They snapped their heads and stared at each other in disbelief. "Blasphemy!" the one whispered. The other echoed the charge in a louder voice, "Blasphemy! Who is he to forgive sins? Blasphemy! Only God can forgive sins, not this man. Who does he think he is, anyway?"

Nobody else said a thing. Every eye was fixed on Jesus. Slowly Jesus' eyes smiled, and then his lips smiled too as his gaze found the two scribes among the inside group. His head fell back and he laughed.

"I hear you. I hear what you say." Jesus' voice was light but firm. "You miss the point completely. What should I say, 'Your sins are forgiven' or 'Stand up and take your mat and walk?'†" Jesus laughed again. "You just don't get it. Those who know God's love and compassion also know God's forgiveness." Jesus leaned forward, elbows on his knees. Speaking in a serious tone to the paralyzed man, he exclaimed, "The Son of Man has authority on earth to forgive sins."† And after a moment, Jesus added, "You, child of God, you are whole. Get up. Pick up your mat. Then, walk home."

The cripple hesitated, but Jesus nodded affirmation and urged him on with his hands. Grasping the nearby tabletop and pulling himself up, the man rose onto quaking legs. He looked at Jesus. Jesus nodded again and smiled. "Go. Go home and be well."

The man lifted his left foot and pushed it forward. He reached out and grasped Simon's shoulder, and then swung his right leg forward. Slowly, step by shaky step, the man made his way out of the house and into the crowd. The rope, still snugly tied to his mat, dragged behind him. Atop the roof, the four sons hooted and danced, and then they swung wildly down to the street where their father was.

A buzz started among those in the house. The murmur quickened, traveling through the crowd much faster than the once paralyzed man could ever hope to run. "Incredible! Nothing like this has ever been seen before!" the people said.

In the town of Capernaum, near the top of the Sea of Galilee, the summer days were hot, though occasionally a cooling breeze came off the open water. One day forty or fifty people followed Jesus across the stony beach to the shore. As he walked, he taught those with him about God's steadfast love.

Later, on their way back to town, Jesus and the crowd came upon Levi, who was Alphaeus's son. Levi was a tax collector for the Romans and, because of this, was hated by most of his neighbors. Jesus had known Levi for years. That day Jesus stopped at the tax booth and stood in front of his friend. A boy was playing with a hoop nearby. It wobbled as it rolled, crashing into the booth and then ricocheting into Jesus. He righted it and rolled it to the youngster. Levi watched. "Follow me,"† Jesus said to Levi. "Come on, Levi. It's time to follow me." Levi collected his tax records and bag and stood up next to Jesus. "OK, then. To my house to eat and talk," he said.

Dinner that night at Levi's house was a raucous affair with good food and plenty of wine. Other tax collectors were there too, along with Jesus' disciples, hangers-on, seekers, a widow, and even two single women—perhaps they were prostitutes. A couple of scribes who worked for the Pharisees were in the house, but they kept a distance. They saw plain as day that this party was a collection of sinners—not only tax collectors but also people who were defiled and impure! They called a disciple away from the table—it was James—and asked, "Why does Jesus eat with all these disreputable people? Why? Doesn't he care about being contaminated by them?"

James slipped back to the table, next to Jesus, and told him what the scribes had asked. Jesus scanned the room. He saw the scribes and beckoned them forward. They took half a step and then stood still. Jesus spoke directly to them. Everybody heard what he said: "People who are well don't need a doctor, right? But if you're sick . . . I'm not so interested in folk who are already righteous." He paused and sipped some wine. The two stared with open mouths. "No," he continued, "I have come to call the disheartened, the broken, and the downcast—those who seem so full of sinfulness to you."

John the Baptizer and his disciples usually fasted. So did the Pharisees. A sincere young man asked Jesus, "How come John's disciples fast, and the Pharisees and their disciples fast, but you and your disciples aren't fasting?" It was a good question, and a lot of people were wondering about that.

As he did more and more often, Jesus responded with an illustration: "At a wedding the guests eat. They don't fast so long as the bridegroom is there, do they?" Those listening nodded, but they didn't really understand why Jesus was talking about a bridegroom. Jesus smiled and continued in a sober tone, "Some day the bridegroom will suddenly be snatched away. Now that's the day to fast!" Faces twisted a bit and eyes wondered.

Jesus' fingers played with his beard. People waited for what he would say next. "OK, look," he continued. "You don't patch an old cloak that's been washed many times with unshrunken cloth. It would be stupid, right? The new patch would pull the cloth apart the first time it was washed, and the tear would be even bigger. Now, do you see what I mean?" They did and yet they didn't. Jesus thought for another moment. "OK, how about this?" He stretched. "No one puts new wine into old wineskins because the skins would break open, and the wine would be wasted just like the skins. No, new wine goes into new wineskins." Faces twisted some more and most eyes still wondered.

It was a few weeks later that Jesus and a band of his disciples were cutting across a grain field. As usual they plucked off some grain heads and ate them. On the far side of the field, a Pharisee and his family were watching. They were keeping the sabbath, so the Pharisee was astounded because it was unlawful both to travel on the sabbath and to glean grain. The sabbath was a day of rest, and what these sinners were doing was considered work.

The Pharisee stood in the way of Jesus, puffed out his chest, pointed a crooked finger, and upbraided him. "Look, why are they doing what is not lawful on the sabbath?"† Jesus listened politely to the harangue. When the Pharisee had repeated himself three times and finally had run out of words, Jesus confronted him: "Have you never read what David did when he and his companions were hungry and in need of food?"†

The Pharisee didn't answer but squirmed under his robe. Jesus' followers came closer so they could hear, and they encircled the Pharisee, his wife, and children. "I'll tell you," Jesus said calmly and directly. "At the time Abiathar was high priest, remember? David, our great King David, went into the Temple and ate the consecrated bread—that Holy food—the bread that was meant only for the priests. And David shared it with everybody who was with him." Jesus looked into the eyes of the Pharisee. He surveyed the faces of his friends. Then he said peacefully, "The sabbath was made for humankind, and not humankind for the sabbath."†

As the words sunk in, the Pharisee had a look of horror on his face. Jesus said one more thing: "So the Son of Man is lord even of the sabbath."† The Pharisee turned on his heels and quickly shepherded his family through the crowd and into his house.

Chapter 3

O N THE SABBATH following Rosh Hashanah, Jesus and his friends returned to the synagogue and passed through the old carved doors. They stepped into the room but stood still for a moment while their eyes adapted to the dim light. Only a few candles atop tall stands lighted the space. A couple dozen men were present, getting ready to sing the psalms and say the prayers.

Jesus wended his way around the perimeter and came upon a man praying alone. One of his hands—his right hand—was palsied. The knuckles were red and swollen; the fingers were crooked and bent in on themselves. His overgrown fingernails were cracked and dirty. The flesh on that hand was withered.

Jesus smiled at the man. "Shalom," he said. The man who had been praying looked up. He, too, said, "Shalom." The man did not know Jesus, nor did he know what Jesus wanted. Jesus said in a normal voice, "Let me see your hand." At this, the others in the synagogue—some were Pharisees who wanted to accuse Jesus of blasphemy—turned with curiosity. There was an unspoken question among them: Would Jesus do what he had been doing all over Galilee and heal this man's hand, even on the sabbath? The synagogue fell silent.

Jesus' left hand reached out cautiously and took hold of the man's withered hand. He held the crooked fingers lightly in his palm and then gently rolled the hand over so he could see the underside. Jesus' thumb slowly rubbed back and forth across the shriveled skin. The man simply watched Jesus. With the deformed hand cupped in his own, Jesus glanced around the room. His voice broke the awkward stillness. "Tell me, friends," he began. "Is it lawful to do good or to do harm on the sabbath, to save life or to kill?"†

Nobody answered. Jesus waited. He surveyed each face. Lowering their gaze, the onlookers squirmed and wiggled as if they couldn't quite get comfortable. They were stuck on his unfair question and stuck in their old ways, afraid to answer wrongly and even more afraid to show compassion. Jesus' brow furrowed. His eyes flashed displeasure toward them.

"Friend." Jesus' eyes slid back to look at the man. He continued. gently to caress the bad hand. "Now," Jesus said softly, "open your hand." The man looked puzzled. Jesus repeated himself, "Open your hand." The cripple looked down at his own hand and, unexpectedly, opened it, just as Jesus had asked.

The man lifted his hand, flexing his fingers wide open and then making a fist. He held his hand in front of his face and twisted his wrist. His disfigured hand worked! Beams of amazed joy brightened his eyes and a wide open grin spread from ear to ear. He looked from his hand to Jesus and back to his hand. Jesus smiled too.

A collective gasp filled the synagogue. The Pharisees were shocked. Healing this man's hand on the sabbath was an abomination and contrary to the Law. They left and immediately went to tell the Herodians, who supported the royal family of Israel under the Romans. If they were to rid themselves of Jesus, to destroy him, they would need official sanction.

Jesus and his disciples left the synagogue and walked the short distance to the sea. When some locals saw Jesus and his friends on the road, they followed. They wondered if something wonderful might happen. The town was full of visitors—from Judea, from Idumea, which is on the other side of the Jordan, and even from as far away as Tyre and Sidon—and they joined the multitude as well. It was like a great parade. The crowd grew large and people were pushing in on Jesus and his disciples. Jesus asked James and John to get a boat ready, which they did. It was their father Zebedee's black cedar and oak fishing boat.

Because Jesus had cured the diseases of many in recent days, various people hoped—or, rather, expected—they would be healed by Jesus if they just touched him. Whenever demons encountered Jesus, they would drop to the ground. Some say the spirits shouted, "You are the Son of God!"† right out loud. Whenever that happened, Jesus told those spirits to be silent—not to make this known about him.

Out of the many, many disciples who had been following him, Jesus called twelve to come with him. Together they set sail and quickly traveled down the coast several miles, around a spit of land and into a sandy cove where they beached the boat. Jesus led these friends up a high hill.

Sitting together beneath some cedar trees on the hill's crest, he told them he wanted their help as apostles—to live together with him, to adopt his way of life, to proclaim the good news, and even to cast out demons themselves. There was Simon (Jesus called him Peter); Zebedee's two sons, James and John (Jesus named them Boanerges, which means Sons of Thunder); Andrew; Philip; Bartholomew; Matthew; Thomas; James, Alphaeus's son; Thaddaeus; Simon, who was a Cananaean; and Judas Iscariot, the one who betrayed Jesus. The twelve agreed.

Afterward, Jesus and his newly appointed apostles went back down the hill and got into Zebedee's boat again. Since the breeze was against them, they had to row back to Capernaum. Though it was late afternoon as they walked from the beach toward home, somehow the crowd rediscovered them and the parade started all over. So many people were pushing and shoving, wanting to get close to Jesus, that they couldn't even get away to eat supper.

Jesus' family heard about the commotion and about Jesus being at the center of it. They were embarrassed and wanted to stop him. People who knew Jesus thought, "He has gone out of his mind."† If that wasn't bad enough, some scribes—wise men all the way from Jerusalem—said, "He is full of Beelzebub—the Devil— and it's only with Satan's help that he gets rid of demons." They also said, "He has an unclean spirit."†

When Jesus learned what was being whispered about him, he faced the foolishness head on. Standing in the midst of the crowd, Jesus asked the scribes to come closer. Four of them, feeling rather bold and powerful, elbowed their way through to where Jesus was. As their eyes met Jesus' eyes, their bravado dissolved. Jesus confronted them this way: "I have a question for you." He paused as they looked at one another. "How can Satan cast out Satan?"† Slowly stroking his beard, he waited for an answer. The scribes exchanged glances. A mother scolded her son. The warm evening breeze danced across the square.

Then Jesus said to everybody, "If a kingdom is divided against itself, that kingdom cannot stand. And if a house is divided against itself, that house will not be able to stand. And if Satan has risen up against himself and is divided, he cannot stand, but his end has come."†

Jesus stopped right there. He examined the four scribes from Jerusalem, who were not looking at him but at their toes. After a full minute, Jesus continued. "No one can enter a strong man's house and plunder his property without first tying up the strong man; then indeed the house can be plundered."† He spoke unequivocally, with absolute confidence. Looking past the scribes at everyone else, Jesus said, "Truly I tell you, people will be forgiven their sins and whatever blasphemies they utter."† Then he looked at the scribes as he continued, "but whoever blasphemes against the Holy Spirit can never have forgiveness, but is guilty of an eternal sin."† The uncomfortable scribes still stared at their feet.

Mary, Jesus' mother, and her children finally arrived, but the crowd was so tightly knit that they couldn't even get to Jesus. Word quickly spread to him that they were there—that he should stop what he was doing right away. A bystander said to Jesus, "Your mother and your brothers and sisters are outside, asking for you."†

Jesus pinched the bridge of his nose, thinking, and brushed a beetle off his shoulder. "And so," he started calmly. "Who are my mother and my brothers?"† He viewed the myriad faces in front of him—old men and young men, women, boys and girls, grandmothers. Head held high, a broad smile on his face, Jesus spread his arms, turning from left to right as if embracing each person and everybody at once. "Here," he said. "Here are my mother and my brothers! Whoever does the will of God is my brother and sister and mother."†

Those near enough to hear were stunned. Like a flood tide, the buzz sped from person to person, eventually reaching even his mother, brothers, and sisters.

Chapter 4

THE AFTERNOON HEAT one fall day drove Jesus to the Sea of Galilee. As always, people flocked to him. He sauntered into the tepid water and waded out several yards. His robe floated at his knees. More people arrived. Some strolled into the water too. Toddlers and children played at the shore's edge. Mothers watched.

Jesus leaned down, cupped his hands in the water, and doused his face. Again and again he splashed himself until his hair and the shoulders of his robe were soaked. And still more people came to the beach.

Soon, hundreds were there—young and old sitting together, children running and playing, women wearing scarves over their heads to shield the hot sun. James and John commandeered a small boat and held it steady while Jesus climbed in. Water dripped from his robe and hair. There, sitting in the boat with the crowd arced around him on the beach, Jesus taught in his usual way—by telling parables. And while he was teaching that day, this is one of the parables he told:

"Listen! A sower went out to sow. And as he sowed, some seed fell on the path, and the birds came and ate it up. Other seed fell on rocky ground, where it did not have much soil, and it sprang up quickly, since it had no depth of soil. And when the sun rose, it was scorched; and since it had no root, it withered away. Other seed fell among thorns, and the thorns grew up and choked it, and it yielded no grain. Other seed fell into good soil and brought forth grain, growing up and increasing and yielding thirty and sixty and a hundredfold."†

Jesus was excited. He became so animated telling this parable that he nearly fell out of the boat! One moment he was gesturing with his hands and arms, pretending to plant seeds, and the next he was standing up in the tipsy boat, pretending to be a sprouting plant. James and John balanced the craft. They were laughing half the time at the thought of Jesus tumbling into the water.

After Jesus finished the parable about the sower, he sat down and waited a little while. He always looked right into people's eyes. Quite suddenly, he threw back his head and laughed out loud. Then, he snapped his fingers and said, "Let anyone with ears to hear listen!"†

Later, most of the crowd went home for supper. Jesus now stood on the beach, talking with the twelve and a few others who had stayed. A woman in the crowd raised her hand. She asked Jesus why he taught in parables and what they meant.

Jesus ran his long fingers through his hair. He sat down on a driftwood log, and the others gathered around. He took a deep breath. "Look," he began. "To you has been given the secret of the kingdom of God, but for those outside, everything comes in parables; in order that 'they may indeed look, but not perceive, and may indeed listen, but not understand; so that they may not turn again and be forgiven.'"† Jesus put a finger to his ear. "Listen," he continued. "You get this parable about the sower, don't you? If you can't figure out this one, you'll never understand any of the others, no matter how many times I tell them."

Then Jesus rubbed his face with both hands. He took another deep breath and gazed up at the golden evening sky. "OK. Now, pay attention," he said. "The sower sows the word. These are the ones on the path where the word is sown: when they hear, Satan immediately comes and takes away the word that is sown in them."† The listeners' faces were agog.

"Then there's a second group," Jesus explained. "These are the ones sown on rocky ground: when they hear the word, they immediately receive it with joy. But they have no root, and endure only for a while; then, when trouble or persecution arises on account of the word, immediately they fall away."† A few heads nodded.

"And others are those sown among the thorns: these are the ones who hear the word, but the cares of the world, and the lure of wealth, and the desire for other things come in and choke the word, and it yields nothing."† More nods.

Jesus put his hands together, with fingers interlaced inside his palms. He continued. "And these are the ones sown on the good soil."† He opened his hands and wiggled his fingers as if they were the ones sown on good soil. "They hear the word and accept it and bear fruit, thirty and sixty and a hundredfold."† Jesus grinned a big, toothy smile and nodded his head, pleased with his explanation. His friends, satisfied, nodded too.

Jesus stood up and took a break. He reached for the water bag and drank, stretched his back, and walked around in a small circle. His friends chatted among themselves. A few minutes later he sat back down on the driftwood. "OK, here are some more things to think about." He asked, "Does it ever make sense to put a lamp under the bushel basket, or under the bed, and not on the lampstand?" He scratched his beard and then added, "For there is nothing hidden, except to be disclosed; nor is anything secret, except to come to light. Let anyone with ears to hear listen!"† And he snapped his fingers again.

Jesus was very relaxed with this small band of followers. The large crowds had not returned, and he patiently taught and answered the questions of those with him. At one point he admonished them, saying, "Pay attention to what you hear; the measure you give will be the measure you get, and still more will be given you."† He went on to explain: "In other words, you get as good as you give. If you don't pay attention, you won't understand. For to those who have—those who comprehend what I'm about and what I'm teaching—they will get more and more and more because the door is opened. And from those who have nothing— those who are ignorant to this message—even what they have, including their detachment from God, will be taken away so that they find themselves more lost than ever."

Jesus, full of energy, kept right on talking. "Now, think about this." He hesitated for a moment, and a smile briefly creased his mouth. "The kingdom of God is as if someone would scatter seed on the ground, and would sleep and rise night and day, and the seed would sprout and grow, he does not know how. The earth produces of itself, first the stalk, then the head, then the full grain in the head. But when the grain is ripe, at once he goes in with his sickle, because the harvest has come."†

Jesus scanned the small group. Some understood; some didn't. He kept teaching. "With what can we compare the kingdom of God, or what parable will we use for it?"† Nobody answered. "Well," he began. "It is like a mustard seed," he told them, holding out his thumb and forefinger as if he had a tiny mustard seed between them, "which, when sown upon the ground"—he pretended to plant the seed—"is the smallest of all the seeds on earth; yet when it is sown it grows up and becomes the greatest of all shrubs, and puts forth large branches"—now he held his arms out as if he were the bush—"so that the birds of the air can make nests in its shade."†

Jesus told parables one after another as best he could so that they would understand him. At other times, when he was alone with the twelve, he explained everything in even more simple terms because some of them were still confused.

As darkness set in, Jesus said to his friends, "Let us go across to the other side."† He was exhausted. The day had been long and hot, and he had been teaching for hours. Jesus and the twelve piled into Zebedee's twenty-six-foot fishing boat. Some other disciples got into other boats, and they followed along too.

Once the boats were on open water, the wind rose and whipped the seas. Rain squalls stormed overhead, and heavy raindrops pelted the crew. Three- and four-foot waves broke against the boats, threatening them. Water poured over the gunnels and across the bow. The night was dark and dangerous. The overloaded boats began to swamp.

Despite the rain, Jesus slouched in the stern, sound asleep on an old wool sack. James woke him because they were about to sink. "Rabbi," he shouted in panic above the wind, "we're all going to die!" The boat rolled and pitched, and water sloshed in the bilge. Everybody was soaked. The oarsmen struggled to keep the boat headed into the wind. Jesus sat up on the narrow bench and looked around. He said nothing while he got his bearings and took stock of the situation. Peter yelled at him, "Come on! Don't you even care?" Andrew shouted too, "What should we do?"

"Calm down, all of you," Jesus said. "Just calm down." Then a most amazing thing happened. Jesus stood up in the boat, lifted his head to the sky, and thrust his face straight into the gale. Sea spray whipped his face and stung his eyes. His stringy hair blew in the wild wind. He held out his arms, palms up to the cloud-filled sky. He was praying. Finally, with complete confidence, he simply spoke these words: "Peace! Be still!"† And just like that, the wind stopped. The Sea of Galilee was as calm as could be.

Jesus returned to the bench. Everybody stared at him. After a moment, he asked them, "Why are you afraid? Have you still no faith?"† Then, he laughed and laughed and asked for some bread and fish and the wineskin. All those with him and in the other boats were astonished. Some said, "That was incredible. Who could have done anything like that? The wind and the sea even do what he says!"

Chapter 5

THE LONG NIGHT that started with blustery wind and heavy seas brightened with the sunrise. Jesus and the others arrived at Gerasene on the east side of the Sea of Galilee. Every bone in every body was stiff and tired from the cramped overnight trip. They were all glad to step out of the boats and onto a long beach nestled beneath high, rocky cliffs. Jesus lifted his hands over his head and stretched. He leaned down and touched his toes to loosen his stiff back muscles. And then, without warning, a wild man dashed out of the tombs that were in the cliffs.

From across the beach, the mostly naked man spied Jesus and came at a dead run straight at him. This man was filled with craziness. His hair was knotted and matted; his body was filthy and covered with scratches, scabs, and scars. His contorted face had menacing, unusual, ice-blue eyes. The man's arms flailed uncontrollably over his head and in front of his face. He smelled of vomit and excrement and garlic.

Everybody had heard the stories—that both at night and during the day the man howled among the tombs and on the high hills around Gerasene. He threw himself down and beat himself with stones. People had tried to restrain him, but chains couldn't even hold him down. The man wasn't particularly big, but he had a giant's strength. He would wrench chains apart and smash shackles to pieces—even though he cut himself to a pulp and got bruised to the bone.

When the demoniac got close to Jesus, the others braced themselves because they thought he would attack. Instead, the man slid on his knees through the beach pebbles and grabbed Jesus' legs. He bowed his head to the ground as if paying homage. Then, an instant later, the man lifted his head and looked up at Jesus towering above him. He bellowed, "What have you to do with me, Jesus, Son of the Most High God?"† He held his hands together and pleaded, "Oh please, please, don't hurt me." Jesus prayed immediately, "Come out of the man, you unclean spirit!"†

With a seasoned parent's kind patience, Jesus touched the man's head. He asked calmly, "What is your name?"† The wild man, breath reeking, shouted back, "My name is Legion; for we are many."† Then, still clinging to Jesus, he buried his head in Jesus' robe and wept—but not for long. Jerking his head back so that his matted hair fell to the ground, the demoniac jumped to his feet and grabbed Jesus by the arms. The man begged and begged Jesus to leave the spirits where they were. In spite of this crazy talk, Jesus understood exactly what was going on inside the man. Jesus studied the wretch and then closed his eyes tightly.

Nearby, on a hillside, a couple thousand pigs were rooting around and feeding. The unclean spirits possessing the wild man screamed at Jesus some more, saying, "There! There!" The man pointed at the pigs. "We'll live in the pigs. Send us there." At once Jesus opened his eyes and said, "Go. Go to the pigs." Right then, those devils fled from the madman and swooped into the herd of pigs.

Now, two thousand is a lot of pigs. Every single one of them became crazed, just as wild as the man had been. They ran in circles, snorting, squealing, and bumping into one another. Finally, like a great whining, screeching torrent, they flowed across the hillside and right over the cliff into the water below. Every one of those pigs drowned.

The bug-eyed swineherds were shocked and angry. They had lost all their pigs. Immediately they ran through the country to the nearby city, telling the people about what had happened to the demoniac and to their pigs. Because it wasn't far and because word spread so fast, people rushed to the hillside to see for themselves what had happened.

When they got there, Jesus was sitting on a stone step with the man who had been possessed. Jesus' disciples were passing around bread for the noon meal. The once-crazed man had washed in the sea and had been given a spare robe. He looked quite presentable and was quietly talking with Jesus, completely sane. This unexpected transformation really frightened the onlookers. The swineherds, who had seen the whole thing, begged Jesus to leave their land because they, too, were terrified.

So, Jesus decided to leave. He stood up and told Zebedee's boys to ready their boat. Jesus, the twelve, and his disciples who came in the other boats gathered their things. At the shoreline, just as Jesus stepped over the gunnels and into the boat, the demoniac who had been cured took hold of Jesus' arm. "Please," he begged. "Let me come with you." Jesus refused. "No. Return to your home and friends. Tell them about God's compassion. Tell them what God has done today. You are well now. Go with God's blessing."

Jesus looked into a peace-filled, though disappointed, face. He reached out his hand and gently squeezed the top of the man's arm as smiles broadened across both men's eyes and faces. Neither had anything more to say. Jesus stepped into the boat.

The healed man returned to his home in the Decapolis. He told anybody who would listen about Jesus and what had happened. Those who heard his story were absolutely amazed.

Once again Jesus and his comrades crossed the sea back to the western shore near Magdala. When they arrived, people quickly learned that Jesus had returned. Soon another great crowd came to see him. Among them was a leading member of the local synagogue. His name was Jairus. This Jairus was extremely upset. He threw himself at Jesus' feet. Weeping, he begged, "Please, Jesus. Please. It's my young daughter. She's so sick that I know she's going to die. Please come and touch her. Give her your healing, Jesus, so she'll recover."

Jesus crouched down to see Jairus's face. He nodded and offered a reassuring grin. No words were needed. Jairus leapt up. Grabbing Jesus' hand, he hurried off through the streets. The whole crowd swarmed after them.

Now this was a huge throng of people—hundreds and hundreds. One middle-aged woman in the crowd had been plagued by constant bleeding for twelve years. She had seen physicians, but still she bled and bled without stopping. She was always weak. The woman suffered terribly and was getting worse all the time. She knew of Jesus' reputation and his healing powers. She thought to herself, "All I need to do is touch his cloak and I'll become healthy again."

Amid a sea of bumping and shoving people, the woman pushed her way from behind to where Jairus, Jesus, and his disciples were. When she was close, she reached out her hand. Her fingers only brushed Jesus' robe. Remarkably, her body responded instantly. A vibration of light seemed to shoot through her. She knew right away that she was healed.

Immediately too, Jesus was aware that something had happened. The power of God's healing had flowed through him. Jesus stopped dead in his tracks. The crowd piled up behind him in an almost comic fashion. The woman who had touched Jesus' robe was nearly knocked to the ground. Jesus looked around at the pack of people, from one face to another. Everybody stopped talking. They had no idea why Jesus had stopped.

"Who touched my clothes?"† he asked matter-of-factly. Nobody answered. The woman looked at her feet, afraid she had done something very wrong.

Bartholomew replied, "You see the crowd pressing in on you; how can you say, 'Who touched me?' "†

Jesus scanned the crowd some more. The woman was really scared now. She was shaking all over. Because she was so close to Jesus, she couldn't avoid him. He looked right into her eyes. At that, she fell onto the ground in a heap next to him. She was crying so hard that she couldn't catch her breath. Jesus stood and waited. He gently laid his hand on her covered head. Once she had calmed down, she told him exactly what had happened.

Standing over her, Jesus listened quietly to her story. He reached down and took her hand. She stood up. The two stared at each other. She was still frightened. Then she saw the kindness of his eyes. Jesus cupped his hands around the woman's face and held her gently. "Daughter, your faith has made you well; go in peace, and be healed of your disease."† As usual, he smiled. She hesitated, and then she beamed. She threw her arms around his neck and squeezed. She bathed in the roughness of his robe, breathing in every smell—even the odor of sweat-soiled wool.

The woman's "Thank you" had hardly fallen on Jesus' ears when some neighbors of Jairus ran down the street. They pushed in toward Jairus, and one said in a loud voice, "We've just come from your house, Jairus." Jairus looked stunned. "Your daughter is dead. Why trouble the teacher any further?"†

Jesus, of course, heard this too. He turned to Jairus. "Don't be afraid, my friend. This is the time to believe." Then Jesus told the crowd to disperse. Reluctantly, they wandered away. Jesus brought only Peter, James, and John, along with Jairus, to the house where the child was.

As they turned the corner onto the street where Jairus lived, a ruckus came from the last house on the right—Jairus's house. Family and friends were weeping and wailing. Jesus and the others walked into the house. The women there looked at them, tears streaking their faces. Jesus asked, "Why do you make a commotion and weep? The child is not dead but sleeping."† The women snickered at the notion and then sobbed all the more. So, Jesus told them to go outside and wait.

Jesus, his three disciples, the girl's mother, and Jairus went into the room where the child lay. Sure enough, she looked to be dead.

Jesus went to her bedside. He sat on the edge. The girl's face was peaceful. Jesus stroked her dark hair. He held her hand and closed his eyes. A minute passed. Two. The ever present flies buzzed in the silence. Peter's stomach gurgled. Jairus cleared his throat nervously, and his wife sobbed. Finally, Jesus opened his eyes and simply said in a normal voice, "Talitha cum," which means, "Little girl, get up!"† And that's what she did. The girl heard Jesus and sat right up. She looked around, saw her mother, and took two steps straight to her. Jairus's wife, surprised at her twelve-year-old daughter's instant recovery, hugged the girl. Tears streamed from Jairus's wide eyes, and he wiped the tears from his cheeks.

Pleased, Jesus said to the parents and the child, "What just happened is just between us. Don't tell anyone else. And give the child something to eat. She's very hungry."

Chapter 6

JESUS, JAMES, JOHN, and Peter left Jairus's house. They joined the other disciples in the still-crowded street, for Jesus' followers had not completely dispersed. Questions buzzed among the swarm of people. They wanted to know what had happened to Jairus's daughter.

Meanwhile, Jesus and his friends quietly headed west, dust puffs following each footstep. A small cloud of dust marked the group's progress along the well-traveled road.

Two days later, Jesus and his cohort of disciples rested in Jesus' hometown, Nazareth. On Saturday morning they went to synagogue. "Shalom," the faithful greeted one another kindly. Oil lamps and a few candles were lighted, prayers were spoken, the psalms of David were sung, and the Torah was unrolled and read. One very old man fell into a snoreless sleep right away. His light blue prayer shawl slipped off his shoulder.

When the time came for the teaching, Jesus rose to speak. He faced the twenty-five or thirty bearded, weathered faces that were trained on him. Jesus' voice was gentle, quiet, and confident. He spoke with insight, compassion, and a new wisdom that soaked into those in the silent synagogue.

As Jesus commented on the Torah, he absently fingered the knots on his prayer shawl. From time to time, he swept his black hair behind his ears. Occasionally he paused and looked over the tops of the curious heads, remembering the many times he had worshiped in that place. During one of these interludes, a round-bellied, bald man with gravel in his voice whispered to his neighbor, "Where did this man get all this?"† His not-so-quiet question inspired others. A fellow with a missing front tooth and a scar on his cheek wondered aloud to nobody in particular, "What is this wisdom that has been given to him?"† Somebody who knew Jesus' reputation as a healer exclaimed, "What deeds of power are being done by his hands!"† And finally, one rather disgusted voice grunted, "Is not this the carpenter, the son of Mary and brother of James and Joses and Judas and Simon, and are not his sisters here with us?"†

With this last comment, an air of suspicion and disapproval infused the small congregation. The mood in the synagogue skidded from awe and interest to suspicion and rejection. Many of those gathered—though not Jesus' friends—were offended and harrumphed back and forth rudely with one another about Jesus and what he was saying. Jesus watched and listened passively. His eyes tracked the whispers.

Suddenly, like a heavy, wet cloak, a complete hush fell over the room. Once more, all eyes found Jesus, who was still standing in front of them. He looked from one person to another and held the silence much longer than was comfortable. Some heads dropped and some people fidgeted. Then Jesus began plainly, "Prophets are not without honor."† He hesitated. Eyes darted around, and quizzical faces turned to each other and back to Jesus. Speaking very slowly, Jesus repeated what he had just said, "Prophets . . . are . . . not . . . without . . . honor,"† and then he continued at a normal pace, "except in their hometown, and among their own kin, and in their own house."†

As his meaning settled in the minds of those men, Jesus put his hands on his hips. An I-love-you-anyway expression washed across his face. The townsfolk didn't move when Jesus quietly walked out of the synagogue. His friends followed. As soon as he had gone, those left behind all talked at once about Jesus, what he had said, and what they had seen.

So, in those few days at home, Jesus accomplished very little. As he went among the local villages teaching, he did cure some sick people who were eager for his healing touch; but this was a dry time for Jesus. He was shocked that so many of his boyhood friends and neighbors did not believe. There was a certain sadness on Jesus' face, and he didn't eat or sleep well for several days.

Ten days later, back in Magdala, Jesus excitedly clapped his hands to call the twelve apostles together. He had an idea. Sitting cross-legged on the ground by a rock wall surrounding a vineyard, Jesus told the twelve that he wanted them to visit the people of the countryside in groups of two. John elbowed James, who turned and saw John's finger pointing back and forth between himself and his brother. James acknowledged the request with a quick nod. Jesus continued. He said they would have power over demons. He told them to heal the sick; to travel light, taking nothing but a staff: no food, no sack, no coins, and no change of clothes; and to wear only a tunic and sandals on their feet.

When he had finished these initial instructions, Jesus told the twelve: "Wherever you enter a house, stay there until you leave the place. If any place will not welcome you and they refuse to hear you, as you leave, shake off the dust that is on your feet as a testimony against them."†

Nearly every disciple had a question or two. In answer, Jesus just repeated what he had said before: travel light, heal the sick, stay in one place. The disciples paired up—James and John together, of course—and Jesus sent them on their way. Jesus then had time to himself to think, pray, rest, and relax.

The disciples went throughout the district as Jesus had instructed. They called hundreds of people to repentance, cast out demons, laid hands on the sick and anointed them. Many, many people were cured in those days.

King Herod had heard of Jesus' teachings and of his disciples' healing mission in the countryside. Jesus had quite a reputation, both good and not so good. Some folks even claimed this about Jesus: "John the baptizer has been raised from the dead; and for this reason these powers are at work in him."† And then there were those who thought, "It is Elijah," and still others wondered if Jesus might be "a prophet, like one of the prophets of old."†

When news of Jesus, including all the rumors about him, reached Herod, Herod said, "John, whom I beheaded, has been raised."†

It was Herod himself, you see, who had sent his soldiers to arrest John. And they did just that, binding him and throwing him in prison because Herod's wife, Herodias, demanded it. John had criticized Herod for marrying the wife of Philip, his brother, and that had set Herodias into a fury. John had said to Herod, "It is not lawful for you to have your brother's wife."†

Anyway, Herodias held a grudge against John. She hated him and wanted him killed. Herod, however, was quite afraid of John, who was very popular among the people. He also knew that John was an upright and holy person. In fact, Herod actually protected John for a while. When Herod heard John speak, he was puzzled and impressed at the same time.

Well, Herodias got her way. Herod had a birthday banquet with his courtiers, the officers of the guard, and some other leaders of his kingdom. He got quite drunk. At the party, his stepdaughter danced a very provocative dance. Herod was thrilled. His guests loved the dance too. So, Herod called the girl over and boasted to her in a loud voice that everybody could hear, "Ask me for whatever you wish, and I will give it . . . even half of my kingdom."†

The girl rushed out of the banquet hall and dashed to her mother, who was in a room nearby. The girl told the woman that the dance was great. Everybody liked it. Then she told her what Herod had said, that she could ask for anything as a reward. Innocently, she wondered out loud, "What should I ask for?"† And in that moment, Herodias knew exactly! She rubbed her hands together and replied in a syrupy voice, "The head of John the baptizer."†

Immediately the young girl returned to Herod's banquet. When she reached her stepfather, she blurted out, "I want you to give me at once the head of John the Baptist on a platter."†

Herod was taken aback. His eyes flashed and he asked, "What?" Sweat covered his fat face and dripped from under his arms. His shoulder started to twitch as it always did when he was uncomfortable. He looked around the room nervously. Herod respected John, though he didn't really understand him. And he was afraid of the people, John's disciples. But he was king and had made his oath—and in public too. He couldn't refuse even though this request was terrible. He grabbed his goblet and swallowed all the wine in it.

Right then, Herod called a soldier of the guard. The man came to quick attention. Herod gave the order boisterously and arrogantly for John to be killed: "Get the head of John the Baptist for me right now, and put it on a plate." He wiped the sweat from his face with his napkin.

That soldier went to the prison, which was not far away. He unlocked the cell where John was being held and kicked the door open. John stood up. He took a step to the middle of the room to meet the visitor. Without a word, the soldier, who had already drawn his broad sword, beheaded John with one swift thwack. John's body crumpled in a heap. The soldier snatched John's head by his long, unkempt hair and carried it back to the banquet hall.

When the soldier got to the palace again, he grabbed a serving tray and dumped the food on the table. Then he put John's bloody head on the tray instead. The scene was foul. Some guests were fascinated; some were revolted. The soldier approached the girl with the platter containing John's severed head. He bowed politely and gave it to the girl. She squirmed and looked at Herod. His shoulder twitched. He half laughed as he wrung his hands.

His stepdaughter looked at her own clean hands. Herod nodded to her to take the prize. The girl's stomach convulsed, and vomit rose in her throat. She took the platter and held it against her soft belly. Red ribbons of blood spilled from the platter down her thin, white gown. The platter and head were heavy. The girl couldn't look at her cargo. She quickly left the banquet hall and took the mess to her mother. When Herodias, Herod's wife, saw the girl and her reward, she threw her head back, clapped her hands, and cackled. The girl's stomach convulsed, and she was sick.

Later, when his disciples heard that John had been executed, they came to the prison, got what was left of their friend, and buried him.

After two weeks on the road, the twelve returned to the vineyard near Magdala and met up with Jesus. They talked excitedly all at once, telling what had happened in Nain, Tiberias, Magdala, Cana, Nazareth, Meggido, Beth Shan, and elsewhere. Jesus covered his ears and then held up his hands. Eventually they stopped talking. Jesus laughed. They all laughed. So, two by two the disciples retold their adventures, saying where they'd gone, with whom they'd stayed, who had accepted them and who hadn't, and whom they had cured.

On the road next to the vineyard, people were coming and going. A lot of folks recognized Jesus, and they invited themselves to join the group. After a while, Jesus and the twelve were hungry, but they couldn't even get away for something to eat. Jesus understood the situation. Clapping his hands together, he said to the twelve, "Come on. You need a rest. Let's go to some quiet place by ourselves." It was a good idea because they were really worn out.

Jesus and the twelve got up and pushed through the crowd. The beach was quite close by. As usual, James and John commandeered a boat. The twelve and Jesus climbed aboard. Four of the group—James, John, Philip, and Bartholomew—set to the oars. They rowed slowly up the coast to the northeast on a calm sea. Jesus, sitting on a bench next to Peter, dragged a hand in the water. The others chatted and relaxed. Thomas slept in the bow. Seagulls swooped near the boat, hoping for a handout.

People had seen them board the boat. So, they just followed along the shore road on foot. In fact, more and more people joined those on the road. They came from all the nearby towns. Well, when Jesus finally went ashore, a great multitude had filled the hillside. There must have been five thousand men, as well as women and children and quite a few teenagers. They were sitting, standing, and milling around on this gently sloping hill by the Sea of Galilee. The crowd seemed like a great flock of untended sheep. And all these souls came for just one reason: Jesus. Jesus was humbled and felt compassion for them. So much for quiet time away with the apostles.

Jesus walked among the thousands. He touched those near him. He taught them as he had so many others in so many other places. He kept moving from group to group, area to area—here for a time, over there for a while. Often, questions were asked. Jesus pulled his fingers through his black hair. Dogs roamed in and out of legs, noses to the ground. Mothers suckled babies. Jesus kneeled and healed a small boy with blisters from a burn. Crows and gulls plied the sky. Teens eyed each other. Toddlers scampered about. Women talked. Men talked. Jesus taught. He taught many things all afternoon.

The day grew late. Jesus' legs ached from standing. He was parched too. Andrew came to Jesus and said, "This is a deserted place, and the hour is now very late; send them away so that they may go into the surrounding country and villages and buy something for themselves to eat."†

But Jesus immediately shot back, with an edge in his voice, "You give them something to eat."† Shocked, Andrew replied defensively, "Are we to go and buy two hundred denarii worth of bread, and give it to them to eat?"†

Jesus, though, was quite serious. He demanded of Andrew, "How many loaves have you? Go and see."† Andrew wandered off with a perplexed and hopeless look on his young face. Six or eight minutes later he returned to Jesus. Andrew simply said, "Five. We have five loaves and two dried fish."

Not deterred even slightly, Jesus called the twelve to him. He told them to ask the people to gather into groups of a hundred or even fifty. While this was happening, Jesus waited patiently. Eventually the crowd understood what Jesus wanted them to do, and they rearranged themselves without the disciples' instructions. This repositioning took more than half an hour.

When almost everyone was settled, Jesus stood in the middle of this mass of hungry people. He held a loaf of bread in his left hand and both fish in his right. At first he didn't say or do anything, and people wondered what was happening. His eyes were closed and he breathed slowly. But then Jesus raised the food and his face to the sky and blessed it. He gave the fish to Andrew and broke the bread into pieces. He tore off a small piece for himself and ate it. Then he told the disciples to give bread and fish to the people. Every single person on the hillside that afternoon—at least five thousand men alone—had enough to eat!

This is true! After everyone had eaten—it was nearly dark by then—the disciples and some others took woven baskets and picked up the leftovers. They wandered over the hillside and in between the people. Incredibly, after they collected all the leftover pieces, there were twelve baskets full of bread and fish.

Now, once the cleanup was done, Jesus sent his disciples to Bethsaida in the boat—this was northeast across the Sea of Galilee—while he said goodbye to the crowd.

Later, Jesus stood knee-deep in the sea. He could just make out the disciples' boat in a patch of bright moonlight heading toward Bethsaida. The crowd had finally left. He was alone again. Jesus scooped up some water and splashed it on his face. As always, it woke him up. He dumped handful after handful on his face and down the back of his neck.

Refreshed, Jesus sloshed out of the surf and across the beach. Moonlight shone across the now deserted hillside. Jesus climbed the embankment, skirted a boulder-strewn gully, and came to the crest of the hill. Once there, he kneeled on the grass and prayed.

After midnight, the weather changed. The moon disappeared. A strong wind whistled across the water and kicked up three-foot waves. Whitecaps broke across the bow of the disciples' boat. Sea spray bit at them. The four rowers pulled hard on the oars. Everyone was awake.

Just then, in the early morning, Jesus—hair and robes flapping in the wind—was walking toward them—actually walking across the sea itself! He could see that the disciples were having a difficult time in the boat. He had meant to walk on by, but Peter caught sight of him. Peter shouted to the others and pointed to the dark, shadowy figure on the water that was actually Jesus. Thinking they were looking at a ghost, the disciples screamed out loud. They were really scared. Jesus, though, spoke up and said, "Wait. It's OK. It's OK. Don't be frightened. It's only me."

Then, Jesus took hold of the boat and carefully stepped over the gunnels. John counter-balanced as the boat tipped and then settled again. Jesus sat between Peter and James. Soon everybody calmed down. The nasty wind calmed down too. This astounded the disciples, especially because the incident happened right after the loaves and fishes episode. The disciples still were dumbfounded at how so many could be fed with so little. Jesus thought they were obstinate—that is, their faith just wasn't strong enough.

When Jesus and the twelve completed their journey, they tied the boat to a tree on the shore of Gennesaret and went ashore. A few people were on the beach and they all knew immediately who Jesus was. Some of them ran to tell family and friends that Jesus had arrived. Not surprisingly, the sick were immediately brought to him.

Jesus traveled about to various villages, cities, and farms in the region. The sick were always laid out in the marketplaces, and they begged to touch Jesus' cloak. Marvelously, those who touched him and the people he touched were healed.

Chapter 7

NOW, A CONTINGENT of Pharisees, along with some scribes from the Temple, had made the long, dusty journey all the way from Jerusalem to see Jesus. It was time for the noon meal when they arrived. Jesus and his friends were in the marketplace. They were given some oat bread, lentils, and figs by merchants who knew them and liked them. The place was crowded. As always, many disciples milled around Jesus.

The Pharisees and scribes, of course, had washed thoroughly after their journey. They came to the market in clean garments and walked with an air of importance. After all, they were religious leaders and Temple scholars. So, this group of ritually pure men wedged into the market to see Jesus. He wasn't hard to find.

Ordinary folks—some from the city and others from the country—filled the market and were eating with Jesus. Pigeons perched on the stall poles, dogs searched for scraps, sheep and goats were tied here and there, and some chickens were caged while others wandered around, pecking the ground. Vendors were selling everything imaginable: bread, fruit, vegetables, honey, cheese, birds and animals, dried fish, cloth, olive oil, wine, trinkets, sandals, rope, water bags, knives—whatever people needed. And there were always a few prostitutes searching for business, even at midday. Flies were everywhere!

The Jerusalem visitors kept their elbows tight to their bodies, not wanting to touch any of the rabble they considered dirty. They screwed up their faces and gasped in disgust at the abomination they saw: A lot of Jesus' disciples were eating without having washed! The dirt and grime on their hands was easy to see. They were definitely defiled according to the Law because Pharisees and observant Jews always washed their hands before eating. That was what the elders did. And they certainly did not consume anything if it had not been thoroughly washed first. Tradition also dictated exactly how food was to be prepared in properly washed bronze cooking pots and serving dishes.

So, completely disgusted, the Pharisee wearing a red robe waved his open hand over his head in the direction of Jesus. Once he had Jesus' attention, the man from Jerusalem whined across the top of the crowd, "Why do your disciples not live according to the tradition of the elders, but eat with defiled hands?"†

Jesus broke a piece of bread from the half loaf he was holding and put it in his mouth. When he finished chewing, he replied to the Pharisee, "Yes. Yes, Isaiah was right about you hypocrites." He was looking right at the man in the red robe. The eyes of the other Pharisees and scribes nearly popped out when they heard what Jesus had said. The bunch of them twittered nervously. The rest of the marketers, accustomed to Jesus' straight talk, waited for Jesus to finish his retort.

Jesus stepped toward the Pharisees and scribes. The crowd opened a pathway. The visitors from Jerusalem edged backward. Jesus' confident voice continued, "People may say good things about me, but in their hearts they're certainly not close to me." He paused again, shifting his shoulders and straightening the neck opening of his robe. "Their worship is empty because they teach human commandments as truth."

Then, Jesus put his hands on his hips and leaned ever-so-slightly toward the Pharisees and scribes. He raised his voice in an acerbic tone: "You have a fine way of rejecting the commandment of God in order to keep your tradition!"† And he waved his hand dismissively before continuing. "For Moses said, 'Honor your father and your mother'; and, 'Whoever speaks evil of father or mother must surely die.' " † The Pharisees and scribes listened as Jesus went on, "But you say that if anyone tells father or mother, 'Whatever support you might have had from me is Corban' (that is, an offering to God)—then you no longer permit doing anything for a father or mother, thus making void the word of God through your tradition that you have handed on. And you do many things like this."†

Jesus' friends, the disciples around him, and some of the merchants nodded to one another and chattered about Jesus' courage to talk like that to those Temple leaders. As he often did in these cases, Jesus looked beyond those addressing him and scanned the eyes of the commoners. He said to the people urgently, "Listen to me, all of you, and understand: there is nothing outside a person that by going in can defile, but the things that come out are what defile."†

The Pharisees and scribes looked at one another and gulped.

Later, when the Pharisees and scribes had left in anger and the crowd had dispersed, Jesus went to where he was staying with his close friends. They were all stuffed into the main room. A woman next to Jesus tugged his sleeve. He turned, and this disciple asked him to explain the parable he had just told to the Temple elders— the one about what goes into the body and what comes out.

Jesus motioned everyone to sit down and get comfortable. He sat too, crossed his legs, and held his palms together in front of his face. Looking at each of them he asked, "Then do you also fail to understand?"† Their blank stares said it all. Jesus sighed and rubbed his face. He combed his fingers through his hair and pulled it behind his ears.

"Do you not see," he said with frustration but also with a grin, "that whatever goes into a person from outside cannot defile"—he pretended to eat something—"since it enters, not the heart but the stomach, and goes out into the sewer?"† Jesus went on to tell them plainly that all foods are clean and can be eaten without defiling the person.

Jesus then got quite serious. "Look," he began. "It is what comes out of a person that defiles. For it is from within, from the human heart, that evil intentions come: fornication, theft, murder, adultery, avarice, wickedness, deceit, licentiousness, envy, slander, pride, folly. All these evil things come from within, and they defile a person."† The room was silent for a long time. This time the disciples understood.

From the area of Gennesaret where they had been, Jesus led his followers overland to the northwest, all the way to Tyre along the coast. The journey was long—more than thirty miles—and it took several days. When they arrived, Jesus wanted to rest. Hoping not to be noticed, he slipped into the house of a new friend to lie down. But he couldn't escape. A young woman—a Syrophoenician Gentile—came immediately to the house because word had already reached her that Jesus was in Tyre. The woman had a daughter who acted wild, and the mother was beside herself with worry.

This Syrophoenician woman boldly walked through the door unannounced and stood in front of Jesus. He gazed at her with tired eyes and she at him with equally tired eyes. The woman silently brought the palms of her hands together in front of her chest. Tears welled up in her eyes and then poured down her brown face. She covered her mouth because the words just wouldn't come. Sobbing, trying to compose herself, she stood in front of Jesus. Finally, she grasped Jesus' arms firmly with strong hands. She pleaded with him to make her daughter well, to get rid of the demon in her.

Jesus—throat parched, eyes sore from days of walking in the dust, legs aching, stomach empty, peace interrupted—looked at her trembling body. He said offhandedly, "Let the children be fed first, for it is not fair to take the children's food and throw it to the dogs."†

"Sir," the woman said as she let go of Jesus. She held her head high and her shoulders back. She felt Jesus' fatigue. Looking deep into the light of his soul, she responded with compassion for him as well as for her troubled daughter: "even the dogs under the table eat the children's crumbs."†

As if asleep before, Jesus awoke with a start. His own shoulders straightened. A fire burned in the center of his chest. His arms lightened and his legs strengthened. Suddenly, unexpectedly, Jesus saw the incarnation of every mother's sacred love for her child, of his own mother's love for him. With his compassion inflamed again, Jesus put his hands on this Gentile woman's shoulders. He gave her his blessing with simple words: "For saying that, you may go—the demon has left your daughter."† Jesus knew this was true. And when the woman arrived at her home, she found her daughter playing on the floor. The demon was gone!

After several weeks in Tyre and the surrounding area, Jesus and company were headed back toward the Sea of Galilee and into the Decapolis. First, though, they went north through Sidon. One day in a small village along the way, Jesus was resting during the late fall afternoon. A deaf man was brought to him. This was not unusual. In addition to the man's lack of hearing, the poor fellow had an awful speech impediment. All he wanted was for people to understand him clearly.

The three who had brought him to Jesus were all talking at once, begging Jesus to make their kinsman well. They explained that the deaf man had a lot to say. He was always shouting and bothering the neighbors, not to mention them. But the man couldn't even hear them telling him to shut up. In the end, the man's brother said, "Just touch him, Jesus."

Jesus, like he had done so many times before, took the man aside, away from the crowd. They went outside, around the corner, and behind the house.

First Jesus held the man's face in his hands so the two could look at each other. When the deaf man, embarrassed and confused, shouted and tried to break away, Jesus kept holding his face firmly. The man's eyes came back to Jesus' eyes. The poor fellow was really scared. But something in Jesus' face calmed him, and he started to relax, releasing the grip he had had on Jesus' wrists.

Jesus pulled at the man's filthy ears. Then, he slipped his little finger into one ear at a time while pulling down on the lobe with the thumb and forefinger of his other hand. The man was uncomfortable. He didn't like this poking and pulling at all. He became frightened again.

Finally, Jesus let go of his ears. Then, Jesus spat into the palm of his right hand. He rubbed the first two fingers of his left hand in the spit and touched the man's tongue. The deaf man didn't know what to make of this. But Jesus kept going. He looked up to the sky, sighed a great sigh, and then said, " 'Ephphatha,' that is, 'Be opened.' "†

Immediately, as the man stood there with Jesus, his deafness disappeared. He could hear people talking in the house and in the street. He heard a rooster crow. He spoke to Jesus. "I can hear!" he said, and he could hear himself speak. Then he said, "I can speak clearly." The man was astonished. He "whooped" and "hollered" and ran back into the house. Jesus followed. The excited man danced in circles and hugged his family.

Jesus insisted that the man and his kinfolks not go spreading word around about this healing. But, truth be known, they all boasted about what Jesus had done. One of the man's cousins said, "He has done everything well; he even makes the deaf to hear and the mute to speak."† People all over that area were astounded.

Chapter 8

THE DAYLIGHT HOURS shortened steadily on this long journey home. Jesus and his close friends—twenty or thirty of the faithful were always along with the twelve—walked the roads of the Decapolis. Whenever they came to a village, the entourage swelled. People wanted to hear what Jesus had to teach them. So, that's what he did: teach. After a few hours, or sometimes a day or more, the locals would fall away as the disciples and Jesus made their way out of town. Occasionally an especially inspired soul would join Jesus' itinerant group as yet one more loyal disciple.

One day, still in the Decapolis, another huge crowd gathered around Jesus. There were thousands. They had come back every day. This was the third day the crowd had gathered. The place was like a desert. And what food people had brought with them was long gone. Most had emptied their water and wineskins too.

Jesus picked his way through the thicket of bodies. As usual, when he talked and taught, he would touch a head, an outstretched hand, a shoulder. People reached over to touch him too.

Gradually, Jesus' concentration drifted from what he was saying to what he was seeing. He stopped. His brow furrowed. He rubbed his beard and brushed some hair from his eyes. He scanned the ocean of faces. The people were hungry to hear him, but also they hadn't eaten in a long time. Compassion welled up in his own empty stomach. He told those disciples right next to him, "We have been with these people for three days. They're hungry. I can't send them all the way home because they might faint from hunger."

The disciples looked at one another, wondering what they could possibly do. Thaddaeus piped up, "How can one feed these people with bread here in the desert?"† Jesus and the disciples, you see, had little bread and water even for themselves.

But Jesus asked, "How many loaves do you have?"†

They again looked quizzically among themselves, shrugging their shoulders and holding out empty hands. Bartholomew counted. "Seven,"† he said.

Jesus heard Bartholomew's total. Beneath Jesus' whiskers, a faint smile curled the corners of his mouth, and an even brighter smile shone in the corners of his eyes. Jesus asked Bartholomew to bring him the bread.

Jesus took one rather hard, crusted barley loaf in his hands. He was about to give thanks when he interrupted himself. Holding the loaf in one hand, he waved it like a paddle to tell people to sit down. "Sit. Please. Everybody, sit." Only after the people were settled did Jesus raise the bread and his eyes to the sky. His mouth recited an ancient blessing—"Blessed be God, sovereign of the universe, who brings forth bread from the earth"—but only a few could hear what he said.

When he had finished the blessing, Jesus tore apart the one loaf he held. He took a piece for himself and gave the rest to Bartholomew. He told him to give bread to everybody.

Bartholomew looked at Jesus with a *how can this be?* expression but didn't say anything. So, the rest of the loaves were broken into chunks too. Disciples stepped over and around and through the people and gave a piece to everyone there. Eager hands reached for a bite to eat.

Just as the bread was being passed around, Thomas and Philip stepped forward with a few small fish. They had been sun dried and salted. Jesus took the fish and looked them over. He smelled them and ever-so-slightly nodded approval. Then, he held them up like he had the bread. Again he blessed the food. When he was done, he pulled off a flake of fish for himself because he was still famished.

So, on that afternoon, everybody there ate bread and bits of fish. It was like a great feast! It took more than an hour to pass around the food. When the eating was done, Jesus sent the disciples back into the crowd with baskets to pick up the scraps. People helped, tossing bits and pieces into the baskets as they came by. After the disciples had finished, seven full baskets sat on the ground by Jesus. The disciples were amazed since there must have been at least four thousand there that day.

Everybody, including Jesus, was exhausted, especially in the hot afternoon sun. Finally, he told the people it was time to go home, and they did.

When the last stragglers left, Jesus immediately went to the shore. As requested, James and John had commandeered another boat. Jesus hopped in, along with the twelve. They rowed out and headed south, down the coast to the Dalmanutha district, which is where Magdala is. When they put ashore, Jesus walked from the water's edge to the town.

Word had already spread that it was Jesus and his friends who had beached the boat. Four Pharisees quickly came out to confront Jesus. They wanted to argue. They insisted on Jesus sending them a sign—a sign from heaven—that he, Jesus, had a direct connection to God. He hated these silly games, these petty tests, and he rolled his eyes.

Refocusing, he looked straight at the four, and asked, "Why does this generation ask for a sign? Truly I tell you, no sign will be given to this generation."† With that, Jesus turned and walked right back to the boat. He climbed in again, and everybody followed. James pushed them out into the deep water and then hopped in. They went across the Sea of Galilee to the other side.

Now once again there wasn't much food for the journey—only one loaf in the crowded boat for everybody. Four men were at the oars. The others sat on the benches. Jesus rested quietly in the stern of the boat. He was tying knots in a spare line and thinking. Then, out of the blue, he said, "Watch out—beware of the yeast of the Pharisees and the yeast of Herod."†

What that meant, nobody knew. Thomas whispered to Thaddaeus, "We forgot to bring bread. That's why he said that." But Jesus picked up on the comment. "Why are you talking about having no bread? Do you still not perceive or understand?"† He looked at them with frustration. "Are you just dense?"

Jesus was bewildered that they didn't understand. The rowers stopped. The boat rocked gently. Jesus looked at his friends. "Do you have eyes, and fail to see? Do you have ears, and fail to hear? And do you not remember?"† He paused to let the questions sink in, even though he didn't expect anyone to answer. Then he asked, "When I broke the five loaves for the five thousand, how many baskets full of broken pieces did you collect?"†

"Twelve," they said together.

Jesus persisted, still frustrated. "And the seven for the four thousand, how many baskets full of broken pieces did you collect?"†

"Seven," they answered.

Jesus sat on his bench, a passive look on his face. He dragged his hand in the water. Then, he drew it up and splashed the water onto his face. The disciples watched in silence. Finally, he said just loud enough to be heard, "Do you not yet understand?"†

They were heading northeast. After a long row—about twenty miles—and only a short time under sail, the boat and its crew arrived in Bethsaida. Not surprisingly, Jesus was recognized immediately, and the news that he was in town spread quickly. Soon, two men who lived just outside the town rushed to him. They were holding a short, blind man under the armpits. His feet were kicking just above the ground. His head rolled from the sudden jerks. The three nearly bowled Jesus over. The two captors were blathering excitedly, imploring Jesus to touch their younger brother and heal him.

Jesus grabbed one man by the shoulder and snatched the robe of the other. He had to get their attention. But they kept talking. All Jesus could do was to stand there and hold on. After a while, the two men quit yelling and let go of their blind brother. Jesus smiled.

The poor blind man was totally confused and frightened. Jesus reached out his hand and took hold of the man's hand. He spoke to him gently and put his hand on the blind man's chest. This calmed him down. Then, still holding the man's hand, Jesus led him straight out of the village and away from everybody else.

Once clear of the brothers and the disciples—they were a hundred yards away—Jesus stopped the blind man next to a sheepfold. He took the boyish face in his rough hands and looked into vacant eyes. Then Jesus spit onto the tips of his fingers and wiped the saliva on the eyes of the blind man. The young man pulled back reflexively, shocked by the wetness. Jesus put both hands around the man's face again.

"Can you see anything?"† Jesus asked.

The man looked back down the street and answered, "I can see people, but they look like trees, walking."†

Jesus spit again onto his fingertips and again rubbed the spit on the man's eyes. This time Jesus peered intently into the man's brightening eyes. A minute or two passed. The man blinked a lot. His eyes became moist, then teary. A grin started on the man's face until, finally, it burst into an ear-to-ear smile. He tried to talk but couldn't. He could, however, see perfectly. Jesus smiled too and said firmly, "Now, you go straight home." And, that's what the man tried to do, except he was lost until his delighted brothers found him and showed him the way.

Next, Jesus and his friends went cross-country almost due north to towns around Caesarea Philippi. This was more than a twenty-mile hike, and so there was plenty of time to talk along the way. Jesus was surrounded by the twelve when he asked a curious question: "Who do people say that I am?"†

Without so much as a second of reflection, James, son of Alphaeus, barked, "John the Baptist."† Simon the Cananaean said, "Elijah."† And Andrew piped in, "Some people insist you must be a prophet."

Jesus stopped dead in his tracks. The others stopped. He turned and faced the disciples. Jesus rubbed his beard and pulled his hand through his hair. "But who do you say that I am?"†

They stared at him like wooden posts. But then Peter blurted out, "You are the Messiah."†

"Hum," was Jesus' first reaction. He said it again, "Hum." Then, ever so calmly, Jesus ordered, "Don't say a word about this to anybody."

In that moment, something changed. The air changed. The feel of the ground under their feet changed. The energy between them changed. Something in Jesus changed. Something in what they were all about changed. In fact, right then and there Jesus told them that the Son of Man—that was the term he used—would suffer greatly. He said the elders, the chief priests, and the scribes would reject the Son of Man and then kill him. He added something quite strange, however. Jesus said that three days after the Son of Man is killed, he would rise again. Jesus was not secretive about this at all, but very open. The disciples looked at Jesus and one another. They were bewildered.

Peter quickly slipped over to Jesus' side and took hold of his arm. He pulled Jesus off the road so they were alone. And then Peter poked his finger at Jesus' chest and scolded him for what he'd said about getting killed. Jesus was not pleased. He didn't even let Peter finish. He yanked his arm out of Peter's grasp and turned back to the others. His face was flushed and his eyes narrowed. Peter fidgeted. He was confused and hurt, but Jesus wouldn't let him get away with his arrogance. He dressed Peter down: "Get behind me, Satan!"† Jesus stepped past Peter and continued, "For you are setting your mind not on divine things but on human things."†

Right then Jesus gathered everybody together in the middle of the road under the winter sky. He announced in a serious voice, "If any want to become my followers, let them deny themselves and take up their cross and follow me."† Most faces looked puzzled. The disciples were frightened at how commanding and serious

Jesus was. He continued, "Remember, if you try to save your life, you'll only lose it; but if you lose your life for me and the good news, you'll actually save it." At this, the disciples looked to one another. Some grasped each other's sleeves. There was a growing confusion and concern.

Jesus pushed on. Still in a very sober tone, he asked, "For what will it profit them to gain the whole world and forfeit their life? Indeed, what can they give in return for their life? Those who are ashamed of me and of my words in this adulterous and sinful generation, of them the Son of Man will also be ashamed when he comes in the glory of his Father with the holy angels."†

The disciples gasped.

Chapter 9

L ATE THAT NIGHT, under a sparkling, starry sky, Jesus finished his teaching this way: "Truly I tell you, there are some standing here who will not taste death until they see that the kingdom of God has come with power."† Those who heard Jesus say these things didn't know quite what to think.

Almost a week later, Jesus and his troupe were still in the hilly north country. Jesus needed a break. He wanted to get away. A high mountain was nearby, and Jesus tapped Peter, James, and John to climb it with him. They left before dawn on a cloudy day. Jesus had told the others the night before to expect them back by midday. The group trudged across a narrow valley and up the rugged mountainside. The hike wasn't particularly long, but it was rough. By the time the four reached the summit, they were hot, sweaty, and tired. James, John, and Peter flopped on the ground, exhausted. Jesus walked to the cliff's edge. He looked east into shards of morning sunlight slicing through the low, gray clouds.

Just then, up on that mountain, some astonishing things happened. Peter, John, and James were stunned by them. First, Jesus' appearance changed right before the disciples' eyes. There he stood on the mountaintop as if the blazing white sunlight had electrified him and made his whole *Being* shimmer with brilliance. Even Jesus' dirty brown robe dazzled white—whiter than a new robe bleached by two days in the hottest sun. What the disciples saw was astounding.

As if that wasn't enough, suddenly the images of Elijah and Moses appeared with Jesus. The three were standing by the ledge and talking as if they were old friends. The other three—Peter, James, and John—looked at each other with wide eyes. Their jaws dropped. A bug actually flew into Peter's mouth, and he had to spit it out. But Jesus, Moses, and Elijah stood right in front of them—as real as life. Peter jumped up eagerly and bellowed, "Rabbi, it is good for us to be here."† He had no idea what he was saying. "Let us make three dwellings, one for you, one for Moses, and one for Elijah."†

In the moment that followed, a perfect harmony occurred in the crystal silence and vivid whiteness of cloud-split sunlight. Nobody spoke. Nobody moved. Peter was terrified. Slowly the cloud itself enveloped the mountain, and they were all within it. The temperature dropped, and a light breeze crossed the mountain peak. What happened next was unmistakable. A commanding but sweet voice declared, "This is my Son, the Beloved; listen to him!"†

After that, Peter, James, and John awoke from the vision. What they saw on the ledge was Jesus all alone. The others were gone. But Moses and Elijah had been just as real as the mountain itself. And the voice had been real too.

James brought the water bag to his mouth and drank. He passed it to the others. Jesus drank too. Nobody knew what to say or even what to do. An extraordinary event had occurred.

Jesus seemed content. He beckoned his three friends, and they followed him back down the mountainside. About halfway to the bottom, Jesus stopped. He leaned on a boulder while John, the last in line, caught up. He had to say something because he sensed the awe that James, Peter, and John were feeling. Rather than explain the experience, Jesus cautioned them not to say anything about the vision until—and he used *that* phrase again—"the Son of Man had risen from the dead."† The disciples couldn't believe what had happened themselves, so they kept quiet—though they continued to wonder silently what Jesus meant when he talked about rising from the dead. When they regained the flat land, James couldn't hold back his curiosity anymore, and he asked Jesus, "Why do the scribes say that Elijah must come first?"†

Jesus stopped to answer. His reply was a bit strange. "Well, Elijah does come first. So, how do you suppose, then, that the Son of Man suffers and is tortured? But, I tell you, Elijah has already come and gone. And he was persecuted just as the scriptures say."

James was not satisfied. Nor were Peter and John. Jesus had changed. They wondered what was going to happen next.

The four walked in silence across the rocky valley and up to where the other disciples were. From a distance they could see that another big crowd had gathered. Some scribes were among them, arguing with the disciples. Suddenly a young man, who wasn't paying any attention to the bantering among the people, noticed Jesus, Peter, James, and John approaching. He shouted that Jesus was coming. The crowd immediately broke and ran a hundred yards up the path to greet them. With everybody surrounding them and six or eight people talking at once, Jesus quietly asked what all the arguing was about.

An older man, his head lowered, didn't answer Jesus' question but, instead, pleaded, "Teacher, I brought you my son; he has a spirit that makes him unable to speak; and whenever it seizes him, it dashes him down; and he foams and grinds his teeth and becomes rigid; and I asked your disciples to cast it out, but they could not do so."† The man, shaking his hands in the air, was at his wit's end.

Jesus studied the man's face and posture. His sadness and frustration were palpable. "You faithless generation,"† Jesus said to everybody in a loud voice. "How much longer must I be among you? How much longer must I put up with you?"† Jesus reached out to the man and touched his sleeve. "Bring him to me,"† he said softly. The old man disappeared into the crowd.

Jesus and the flock of people returned to where they had been staying. After ten minutes or so, the father reappeared, holding the boy's hand tightly. As they pushed through the swarm around Jesus, the youngster was suddenly thrown into a convulsion. His eyes rolled back in his head, his mouth foamed, and he gurgled with every breath. The child's arms flailed so much that his father had to let go of him. The boy dropped to the ground—a torturous, flopping mass. People jumped back. Jesus stepped forward. He looked at the boy's father and asked, "How long has this been happening to him?"†

"From childhood,"† the man began. "It has often cast him into the fire and into the water, to destroy him; but if you are able to do anything, have pity on us and help us."† The father's cracked and dirty hands were palms together as in prayer.

Jesus had a slight edge to his voice. His eyes opened wide and he exclaimed, "If you are able!—All things can be done for the one who believes."†

The father's eyes blazed white and wide. He lurched toward Jesus, arms in the air, and shouted, "I believe."† Tears muddied his cheeks. He stared right at Jesus and said directly, "Help my unbelief!"†

People from the inner edges of the crowd pressed in so they could see better. Jesus motioned them back. He dropped to one knee and took hold of the boy's arm. He put his other hand on the boy's hip. The youngster's thrashing stopped. Jesus closed his eyes and prayed loudly, "You spirit that keeps this boy from speaking and hearing, I command you, come out of him, and never enter him again!"† Jesus kept his hands on the child.

Just then, the boy made a deathly cry. His whole body shook spasmodically and went rigid. There he was—splayed on the dirt, drool sliding from the corner of his pale lips. By the look of it, the child was stone dead, a corpse. A loud murmur rumbled through the crowd. "The boy's dead!"

Still on one knee, Jesus took the boy's hand in his own and held it gently for a minute or so. He kissed it. Nobody said a word. Eyes darted from the stone-still boy to Jesus and back. Everybody waited to see what would happen. A light breeze blew across the plain.

Then, Jesus simply stood up and lifted the boy by the hand. The youngster rose up as sure and steady as any normal person. Jesus smiled. The boy saw his father and broke from Jesus. He dashed into his father's arms. Joyful tears streaked the man's brown face. Again the crowd filled with murmurs.

While people marveled at the boy's recovery, Jesus and his disciples slipped into the nearby house to collect themselves. Philip asked, "Why couldn't we get that demon out?"

Jesus looked at him and said in an offhand way, "This kind can come out only through prayer."†

Jesus and his tribe of disciples left the area of Caesarea Philippi and headed south, through Galilee. They kept moving to stay warm as midwinter cold gripped the hill country. Steering clear of villages and crowds, Jesus taught his friends about what was to come. He said those confusing words again, "The Son of Man is to be betrayed into human hands, and they will kill him, and three days after being killed, he will rise again."† Although his followers heard what he said, they were too bewildered and frightened to say anything.

Finally Jesus and everybody else with him arrived back in Capernaum. Once settled in the house, Jesus asked, "What were you arguing about on the way?"† Silence. Nobody wanted to admit what they had been talking about, which was who among them was the greatest.

Jesus sat down. The disciples circled around him and sat too. They knew to pay attention. Jesus said something he'd said many times before, but evidently he needed to say it again: "Whoever wants to be first must be last of all and servant of all."†

As Jesus was talking, one of the children of the house, a toddler, wandered in, thumb securely in his mouth. Jesus reached out and tickled the boy under the arms. He wiggled. Jesus quickly swooped him off his feet and pulled him onto his lap. The child giggled and took hold of Jesus' beard. Jesus smooshed his face into the boy's pudgy belly, and the youngster laughed, letting go of the whiskers.

Still hugging the boy, Jesus returned his attention to the adults. "Whoever welcomes one such child in my name welcomes me, and whoever welcomes me welcomes not me but the one who sent me."†

Though Jesus was having fun with the child, the disciples knew this was serious teaching. John said, "Teacher, we saw someone casting out demons in your name, and we tried to stop him, because he was not following us."†

Jesus magically produced a dried date from behind the youngster's ear, and he gave it to the boy. Without missing a beat, he replied, "Do not stop him; for no one who does a deed of power in my name will be able soon afterward to speak evil of me. Whoever is not against us is for us. For truly I tell you, whoever gives you a cup of water to drink because you bear the name of Christ will by no means lose the reward."†

The disciples looked from one to another, trying to muscle through what they were hearing. Christ? Heads were scratched, faces rubbed, and hands wrung together.

The toddler, thumb back in his mouth, snuggled comfortably into Jesus' lap. Jesus continued. He chose his words carefully. "If any of you put a stumbling block before one of these little ones who believe in me, it would be better for you if a great millstone were hung around your neck and you were thrown into the sea."† Peter ran his hand across the back of his neck.

Next, Jesus held up his hand and said matter-of-factly, "Listen. If your hand causes you problems, cut it off! You're better off one-handed than someone with two hands who goes to hell." Disbelief washed across every single face. "And look," he went on, pushing out his right foot. "If you have a foot that gives you problems, cut it off! You're better lame than standing on two feet in hell." He paused only briefly. "As for your eye, if it brings you trouble, rip it out! You're a lot better with one eye than having two in the unquenchable fires of hell." Evidently this exaggeration served Jesus' purpose. It woke up every one of them and yanked them away from thinking so much about themselves.

Everyone in the crowded room was frozen somewhere between grotesque reality and curious paradox. No one knew what to say. Jesus held them in his gaze until, finally, he finished with this: "Everyone will be salted with fire. Salt is good; but if salt has lost its saltiness, how can you season it? Have salt in yourselves, and be at peace with one another."†

Chapter 10

I N EARLY SPRING, Jesus turned south toward Jerusalem. He and his disciples left Capernaum in Galilee and the north country beyond. They traveled the trade route low in the Jordan River valley. Walking was easy, even pleasant on the seventy-something-mile trek to Judea. And day by day, word spread on ahead that Jesus was coming. Soon there were crowds again. People gathered and gawked. They had heard of this healer-teacher. And whenever he was surrounded by a throng of the curious, Jesus taught them about the good news.

One Tuesday some Pharisees came to hear Jesus. They hovered in a covey on the outskirts of the people. They watched. They listened. After a time, they cackled among themselves until, finally, they agreed to test Jesus with a tricky question. A short, round man with fat cheeks and stubby fingers—the leader of the bunch—shouted in a squeaky voice across the shoulders of those in front of him: "Is it lawful for a man to divorce his wife?"†

Jesus turned to his right and looked into the crowd to see who had asked the question. Olive-brown faces, black beards, dark eyes, the usual dusty, brown wool robes. Everybody looked the same—except for three men in the back with clean faces, wrapped heads, and smirks on their bearded faces. Jesus held his hands together near the bottom of his own beard. His fingers migrated slowly upward until the cracked nails of his two index fingers bracketed his front teeth. He looked at the three. The crowd's idle talk skidded to a hush. Jesus dropped his hands. He gestured, palms open, in their direction as he asked in reply, "What did Moses command you?"†

The short, round Pharisee looked at his cohorts quickly. He rose on tiptoes, pushed his head forward, and answered smugly, "Moses allowed a man to write a certificate of dismissal and to divorce her."†

Jesus took one step toward the men. The people parted like the Red Sea. Jesus took another step. The Pharisees held their ground and stood with confidence and authority. Jesus perused the crowd and then spoke to the three: "Because of your hardness of heart he wrote this commandment for you. But from the beginning of creation, 'God made them male and female.' 'For this reason a man shall leave his father and mother and be joined to his wife, and the two shall become one flesh.' So they are no longer two, but one flesh."† He held out his hands and clapped them together. "Therefore what God has joined together, let no one separate."†

The crowd came together and "swallowed" the Pharisees. Jesus taught in that place for another hour.

Later, when they were having supper in a house nearby, Jesus was asked again about divorce and the law of Moses. This time, he held his hands open, palms up, and said plainly, "Whoever divorces his wife and marries another commits adultery against her; and if she divorces her husband and marries another, she commits adultery."†

Every day more people came looking for Jesus. Mothers often brought their little children. Once, Jesus was lying on his back in the long shadow of some cedar trees. It was one of those times when the children of a whole village were there. Some were in the arms of parents. A gaggle of toddlers was holding hands in a daisy chain. Older kids played with sticks and ran around, wildly yelling at one another. There were screams, laughter, and occasionally some crying. Jesus held his hands behind his head, listening and watching.

Of course, a lot of people who had no children were there too. They wanted to hear what Jesus had to say. But at that moment, it was a play yard of kids. Peter and some other disciples felt cranky about the children being there. The youngsters were a bother, an interruption, an irritation. Two jumped across Jesus' outstretched legs. "Shoo! Away! Leave the teacher alone," Peter said as he tried to sweep the youngsters out of the way. It didn't work. The kids just squirted out of his clumsy grip and popped up elsewhere.

Jesus sat up when he saw what was happening. "Wait. Stay," he told the kids. He turned to the crotchety disciples. He was cross and insistent: "Let the little children come to me; do not stop them."† Jesus persisted, saying, "The kingdom of God belongs to those who are like children."

Jesus scooped up a boy and his little sister. He tousled the boy's curly, black hair. The child jerked his head away and tried to squirm out of Jesus' hug. But he stopped when he heard the clucking noise Jesus was making in the little girl's ear. She pulled her head back and stared at Jesus with surprise and wonder. The mother of these children stepped closer and then sat down near Jesus, just in case they became too rambunctious. Her eyes and Jesus' eyes exchanged a kiss of peace.

By now everybody was watching. Jesus scanned this family of faces and squeezed the two children closer. "Now listen to the truth," he continued. "Anybody who can't accept the kingdom of God as a little child will never get to it."

Jesus looked at these two beauties and kissed them both before letting them go. He smiled, affirming the truth and importance of his message. The children scampered off.

Two days later, Jesus and his friends—the men and women who were usually with him—all set out again, continuing their journey south. Before they had traveled a single mile, a frantic man dashed past the disciples and Jesus, made a hasty pivot on the dusty road in front of them, and dropped to his knees. Everybody jerked to a halt.

The man, his hands clasped in front of him, stared up at Jesus. "Good Teacher,"† he blurted out. "What must I do to inherit eternal life?"†

Jesus began humbly, asking, "Why do you call me good?"† The man's face twisted. He was puzzled. Jesus went on. "No one is good but God alone."†

Jesus studied the man kneeling on the rocks. "You know the commandments,"† he continued seriously. "'You shall not murder; You shall not commit adultery; You shall not steal; You shall not bear false witness; You shall not defraud; Honor your father and mother.'"† The man's face brightened as Jesus recited each commandment. Then he puffed himself up and reported proudly, "Teacher, I have kept all these since my youth."†

Then Jesus kneeled with him on the rocky road. The man looked at Jesus and waited for something wonderful to happen. He had heard the stories. Jesus reached out and put his hands on the man's shoulders. He held the man's eyes with his own eyes. When Jesus opened his mouth, he spoke plainly: "You lack one thing; go, sell what you own, and give the money to the poor, and you will have treasure in heaven; then come, follow me."†

The once hopeful man was crestfallen. His face turned pale. He stared at Jesus but not for long. His eyes dropped, followed by his head. He got up slowly, stiffly, as if his body was hurting. He stepped around Jesus and walked straight through the disciples, back to his home. People knew this disappointed man—this rich man who owned many things—would never get rid of his precious possessions.

Jesus stood up and brushed off his robe. He put his hands to his face and rubbed. Jesus looked at his fellow travelers, standing in the road under the morning sun, and at the man walking away behind them. He said with compassion, "How hard it will be for those who have wealth to enter the kingdom of God!"†

Jesus could tell right away that the disciples didn't understand. A wondering look drifted from face to face. "Children!"† He was slightly annoyed. He raised his voice and persisted, "How hard it is to enter the kingdom of God!"† The disciples were in a fog. He needed an illustration, a metaphor they would remember. Then he snapped his fingers. "It is easier for a camel to go through the eye of a needle than for someone who is rich to enter the kingdom of God."†

The disciples were still blank-faced and somewhat discouraged. The chitchat among them instantly became intense. Some wondered to each other, "Then who can be saved?"†

Obviously, Jesus heard them. He piped in, "It may be impossible for people, but don't forget: for God, everything is possible."

Peter, irritated by Jesus' explanation, hollered at Jesus in one of his exasperated tones, "Look, we have left everything and followed you."†

Jesus understood just how discouraged everyone was. At that moment, most of them truly thought they would never find the grace of God's domain. "Look," Jesus began again. "Truly I tell you, there is no one who has left house or brothers or sisters or mother or father or children or fields, for my sake and for the sake of the good news, who will not receive a hundredfold now in this age—houses, brothers and sisters, mothers and children, and fields with persecutions—and in the age to come eternal life."† Faces lightened a bit. James elbowed John. Things were getting better. Then Jesus repeated the paradox he had said so often: "But many who are first will be last, and the last will be first."† Jesus smiled, satisfied that he had broken through. He turned without another word and stepped onto the dusty road toward Jerusalem.

The band of disciples, including the twelve, hesitated, fused together. They were still unsure of the lesson and concerned for what might happen in Jerusalem. Jesus got out ahead by fifty or sixty yards. Everybody followed slowly. Then, unexpectedly, Jesus walked off the side of the road. He called just for the twelve to come with him, and they did. Jesus did this sometimes. The others patiently waited on the road.

The twelve sat in a bunch, and Jesus sat down too. He spoke very seriously. "You see, we're headed to Jerusalem." They all knew that. Jesus drew a deep breath and said softly, "And the Son of Man will be handed over to the chief priests and the scribes, and they will condemn him to death."† Unease snaked into the group. Throats tightened and some fists clenched. "Then," Jesus continued matter-of-factly, "they will hand him over to the Gentiles; they will mock him, and spit upon him, and flog him, and kill him."†

Jesus stopped. He looked into the eyes of each one of them: Peter, Andrew, James, John, Philip, Bartholomew, Matthew, Thomas, James son of Alphaeus, Thaddaeus, Simon, and finally, Judas. Now the twelve were feeling tense, even agitated. Bodies shifted. Peter fussed the most. Jesus finished: "And after three days he will rise again."† There was a stunned silence. There, he'd said it again.

James and John, Zebedee's sons, broke the spell. They bolted to their feet and together said something like, "Teacher, we want you to do for us whatever we ask of you."†

In the seriousness of the moment, Jesus was taken aback. He looked up at the boys and asked, "What is it you want me to do for you?"†

They puffed up their chests and exchanged glances. James spoke for both: "Grant us to sit, one at your right hand and one at your left, in your glory."† They smiled proudly and looked at each other again with satisfaction. The other ten were disgusted.

Jesus replied soberly, speaking one word distinctly after another: "You do not know what you are asking."† Then he asked: "Are you able to drink the cup that I drink, or be baptized with the baptism that I am baptized with?"†

Still with innocent self-confidence, the brothers answered, "Yes. We can!"

Jesus pierced their eyes with his and peered into the bottom of their souls. He said in a voice never heard by any of them before, "The cup that I drink you will drink; and with the baptism with which I am baptized, you will be baptized; but to sit at my right hand or at my left is not mine to grant, but it is for those for whom it has been prepared."†

Everyone heard this. The others sneered at James and John. But Zebedee's sons held their ground.

Jesus clapped his hands to get everybody's attention again. "Listen," he started. Then, in a torrent of words, Jesus responded: "You know that among the Gentiles those whom they recognize as their rulers lord it over them, and their great ones are tyrants over them. But it is not so among you; but whoever wishes to become great among you must be your servant, and whoever wishes to be first among you must be slave of all. For the Son of Man came not to be served but to serve, and to give his life a ransom for many."† After a full minute of silent reflection, Jesus got up and rejoined the rest of the disciples. The twelve followed.

The journey south now brought Jesus and his faithful group to the foothills below Jericho. They quit the level Jordan valley floor and began the climb up to the city.

A day later, when they were leaving Jericho, they came upon Bartimaeus, a blind man. He was the son of Timaeus and well-known to all the people of Jericho. He sat on the roadside by the city gate. This was his begging place. He had claimed it for many years, ever since he had gone blind.

Bartimaeus, always alert to the comings and goings of travelers and merchants, heard the crowd approaching, going west out of the city. Then somebody said Jesus' name. He listened even more closely and heard another voice say, "It's Jesus." In an instant Bartimaeus pushed away from the wall on his knees, cupped his hands around his mouth, and shouted as loud as he could, "Jesus, Son of David, have mercy on me!"† This was his chance. He knew about this Jesus.

The Jericho townsfolk yelled back. "Shut up." "Be quiet." Bartimaeus was not quiet. He shouted even louder, "Son of David, have mercy on me!"† Jesus couldn't help but hear the man. He could also see him waving his stick in the air as he shouted.

Jesus stopped in his tracks before he reached Bartimaeus. He looked over at the blind man who was trying to get his attention and said, "Tell the man to come here."

Like an undisciplined chorus, those who knew Bartimaeus yelled at him; but poor old Bartimaeus couldn't understand a word because it just sounded like a roar. In a brief niche of silence after the collective shout, a lone voice from the crowd shouted to Bartimaeus, "Take heart; get up, he is calling you."†

Bartimaeus threw off his outer robe, sprang to his feet with stick in hand, and ran to where the voices were. Jesus took Bartimaeus by the hands and asked, "What do you want me to do for you?"†

Bartimaeus was almost out of breath from shouting and running. He lowered his head and shook it slowly, partly to catch his breath and partly in disbelief and anticipation. When he was ready, Bartimaeus lifted his face. He swallowed and straightened his shoulders. He stared with wide open, sightless eyes toward Jesus' voice. "My teacher, let me see again."†

The outer corners of Jesus' eyes narrowed and his cheeks lifted slightly. His lips parted in a smile. Bartimaeus stood quietly—his hands still clasped in Jesus' hands. He waited. He waited in the darkness of the morning light. Then Jesus wrapped his arms around the blind man. He pressed his chest against the chest bones of Bartimaeus. Jesus held him firmly, lovingly. With his mouth in Bartimaeus' greasy hair, Jesus said, "Go; your faith has made you well."†

Jesus broke the embrace, and the two fell apart. Jesus held the man's shoulders at arms' length. Now Bartimaeus looked with clear eyes into Jesus' face in the brightness of the same morning light. Jesus stepped past him and continued on his way.

Bartimaeus followed.

Chapter 11

L ATE ONE AFTERNOON, on the first day of the week before the Passover, Jesus, Mary Magdalene, his close disciples, and the others who had come with them all the way from Galilee arrived at the outskirts of Jerusalem. They were on the road between Bethany and Bethphage. In the distance they could easily see the Mount of Olives a quarter mile from Jerusalem's East Gate.

Jesus stopped. He turned and gently touched the sleeves of Bartholomew and Thomas, who were standing next to him. He had an errand for them. "Go into the village ahead of you,"† he said as he pointed toward Bethphage. "And immediately as you enter it," he continued, "you will find tied there a colt that has never been ridden; untie it and bring it."†

The two started off in the direction of Bethphage. Jesus called after them, "If anyone says to you, 'Why are you doing this?' just say this, 'The Lord needs it and will send it back here immediately.' "†

Bartholomew and Thomas nodded. Sometimes Jesus asked his disciples to do strange things. They were used to his requests.

Andrew offered the waterskin to Jesus. He took it, thanked Andrew, and drank as he drifted to the roadside to sit in the shade. Dribbles of water slithered through his beard. He gave the skin back to Andrew. Others shared their own water too. Some nibbled bread crusts or ate figs. All of them waited for Bartholomew and

Thomas to return. Jesus knocked a fly away from his nose and then closed his eyes. Silence fell over the group.

Bartholomew and Thomas had gotten no more than fifty yards into the village of Bethphage when, sure enough, they saw a colt. It was tied with a rope around its neck to an iron ring next to a door. They had no idea if it had ever been ridden, but it looked pretty young.

A knot of people were talking there in the street outside their homes. Bartholomew and Thomas walked right up to the animal, and Bartholomew started to untie it while Thomas rested his arm across the colt's withers. Three of the bystanders went over to them. The tallest barked, "What are you doing, untying the colt?"† Bartholomew and Thomas spoke at the same time. They said, "The Lord needs it and will send it back here immediately."† The three looked at the two, and then at one another. They seemed satisfied to understand that the colt wasn't being stolen. Bartholomew simply took the rope, wrapped it around the colt's mouth in a loop, and started to lead the animal away, back toward Bethany.

At first the critter came along nicely, but then it got cranky and stopped, digging in its hooves. Bartholomew's arm was straight out behind him as he tugged. Thomas, who knew something about animals, picked up a brittle, brown palm frond and brushed it across the back of the colt's hind legs. Right away the colt was off walking again. After that, whenever the colt slowed down, Thomas lightly touched the back of its legs with the palm frond.

Twenty minutes later—it was less than a mile to where Jesus was—the two disciples were back where they had started. Jesus heard the commotion of their arrival, opened his eyes, and stood up. In three quick steps he met Bartholomew, Thomas, and the colt.

The small, sand-brown donkey stood stock-still—tall, fuzzy ears alert; eyes wide. Jesus put his hands behind the animal's ears and rubbed gently. Then he ran his hands down the colt's long face and across its nose. He noticed the distinct donkey smell. Jesus stepped next to the colt and pressed his hip against its shoulder, where there was a thin, dark brown cross running along its backbone and down its shoulders. As his left hand traced the colt's neck, his right hand pushed down on its rump. He patted it a couple of times and a dust cloud billowed out of the fur. Suddenly, with mouth wide open and teeth biting the air, the donkey hee-hawed. Nobody paid much attention.

Thomas draped his cloak across the animal's rump. Then, Jesus took Thomas's hand to steady himself as he stepped over the colt's back and sat astride the animal's rear. The hind legs of the colt wobbled but quickly found their strength again. All at once, Jesus, the young colt, the men and the women in the entourage, and a gathering crowd stepped forward together. Bartholomew—still holding the rope—led the way toward Bethphage and Jerusalem. Jesus' feet skimmed the ground. A pack of dogs dashed in and out of the people. Everybody started to cheer.

In the time that Bartholomew and Thomas had been gone, word had spread back to Bethany that the man waiting on the side of the road was Jesus. A lot of people had heard of him, and they appeared out of nowhere at the chance to see him. The crowd quickly grew bigger and bigger. Some people waved long, leafy branches they had cut. Pretty soon people had run ahead and thrown their cloaks on the road, which was littered with branches too. The donkey, with Jesus atop its rump, walked right over them. It was quite a festive parade.

Soon, everybody was shouting, "Hosanna! Blessed is the one who comes in the name of the Lord!"† As the hosannas echoed through Bethphage, more and more people came out to see what was happening. A wave of people carried Jesus toward Jerusalem. Hundreds and hundreds yelled, "Hosanna! Blessed is the one who comes in the name of the Lord! Blessed is the coming kingdom of our ancestor David! Hosanna in the highest heaven!"†

This wildly excited crowd marched straight through Bethphage and into Jerusalem, a distance of only about two miles. All of a sudden, people flooded the center of Jerusalem. Jesus got off the colt and left it with Bartholomew. He climbed the Temple Mount, his hands at his sides. Then, standing there, he folded his arms across his chest. His eyes narrowed. Jesus saw who was there and what they were doing. He looked at the setting sun and decided to return to Bethany for the night. The crowd melted away with him out of the city. On the way through Bethphage, Bartholomew tied the colt where he had found it—to the ring by the door.

The following day—it was Monday—Jesus left Bethany for Jerusalem. There were no big crowds that morning, just his usual group of disciples. Jesus was hungry. He hadn't eaten since supper. He noticed a green-leafed fig tree up ahead and wondered if it might have anything on it. When he walked over to the tree, not a single fig was on it. No surprise, though. It wasn't the season for ripe figs. But as he passed by, Jesus spoke to the fig tree. Peter, and maybe some of the others, heard him say, "May no one ever eat fruit from you again."† And they continued on to the city.

Jesus went through Jerusalem's East Gate and onto the Temple Mount. His friends clustered around him. They moved like a swarm of bees. People in the Temple were going about their normal business, mostly ignoring this hive of Galileans.

Jesus stood in front of them—hands on his hips. He watched what was happening in the Temple, which was more a marketplace than a holy place. Men sold pigeons, lambs, and prayer shawls. Booths were set up where Roman coinage was exchanged for Temple currency. The constant activity created a cloud of noise as people shouted, argued, negotiated, accused, and cursed. Jesus listened to the cacophony. He saw Temple guards bossing pilgrims, families pushing and shoving other families, and only a few people praying. From near the Beautiful Gate in the Temple, the chief priests and scribes lorded over all this business.

Without the slightest warning, Jesus flew into a rage. Leaving the others terrified, he bolted, shouting and waving his hands wildly. He grabbed money changers' tables and threw them over. Wood crashed and smashed on the stones. Coins flew in the air and rolled all over the place. People ran away, shouting for this lunatic to leave. Jesus shattered a dozen bird cages, and the sky filled with feathers, squawks, and escaped doves. With teeth gritted and eyes narrowed, he tore through the Temple courtyard like a dervish. It was a melee. Everybody scattered.

After ten long minutes, Jesus stopped and surveyed the damage. Suddenly, the whole courtyard was stone quiet. Jesus was breathless. Sweat rolled off his face, and his robe was wet. His right hand was bleeding. The Temple Mount was a wreck.

While Jesus had been causing havoc, the disciples hadn't moved. They had been too shocked. Jesus raised his hands into the air and screamed in frustration, "Is it not written, 'My house shall be called a house of prayer for all the nations?'"† He turned around in a circle and then shouted again, "But you have made it a den of robbers."† His arms fell to his sides.

When the fracas had started, the chief priests and scribes had stayed on the sidelines. Like everyone else, they had not wanted to get in the way of a berserk man. This Galilean had invaded the

Temple and completely disrupted Temple business. He'd destroyed property and scared people. The elders quickly figured out it was Jesus who had caused all the damage. Then they knew they had to eliminate him, to kill him before he caused any more trouble. Besides, they knew that many were captivated by what Jesus was teaching, a problem even worse than messing up the Temple.

Jesus had gotten everybody's attention. But then, for the rest of the day, he stood in front of the people and taught. At first they were wary, but gradually they settled down and actually listened to his teaching. When evening came, he and his friends left and went back to Bethany.

The next morning, Jesus and the disciples again headed back toward Jerusalem. They took the twisting road from Bethany along the edge of Gethsemane. On the way, they passed by the fig tree Jesus had cursed the day before. It was desiccated, shriveled to the roots.

Shocked, Peter said to Jesus, "Rabbi, look! The fig tree that you cursed has withered."†

Jesus nodded. He reached out and broke off a brittle branch. Everybody watched. Jesus said plainly, "Have faith in God. Truly I tell you, if you say to this mountain, 'Be taken up and thrown into the sea,' and if you do not doubt in your heart, but believe that what you say will come to pass, it will be done for you."† Jesus looked into their friendly faces. He scratched his head and then held out his hands, palms up, still holding the branch. "So I tell you, whatever you ask for in prayer, believe that you have received it, and it will be yours."†

Almost as an afterthought, Jesus said, "Whenever you stand praying, forgive, if you have anything against anyone; so that your Father in heaven may also forgive you your trespasses."†

In silence, they all went up to Jerusalem.

Once in the city, back in the Temple, the chief priests, the scribes, and the elders came up to Jesus. There were about twenty of them. They were red-faced and tight-fisted. Their leader leaned into Jesus' face and demanded, "By what authority are you doing these things? Who gave you this authority to do them?"†

Jesus stood erect. He was calm and confident. A small smile creased his lips and eyes. "I will ask you one question,"† he challenged. "Answer me, and I will tell you by what authority I do these things. Did the baptism of John come from heaven, or was it of human origin? Answer me,"† he demanded.

The Temple elite scurried into a cluster. Instantly they consulted, everyone speaking at once. Then one said clearly, "If we answer, 'John was from heaven,' then he'll ask us, 'Why didn't you take him seriously?'" Somebody else replied, "But what if we say, 'Oh, John was only a person'?" They all knew this was impossible. Because so many people regarded John as a real prophet, this answer would discredit them to people who believed in John.

The chief priests, scribes, and elders dissolved their conference and returned their attention to Jesus. The leader spoke again, "We do not know."† And Jesus said to him defiantly, "Neither will I tell you by what authority I am doing these things."†

The Temple rulers turned and looked at one another, even angrier than before.

Chapter 12

AND SO, JESUS sat on a bench in the Temple that day and he taught those who would listen. The usual noise and commerce were subdued since people worried he might cause trouble again. But the flies still buzzed. Pigeons cooed and sheep and goats called to one another. There was very little breeze. The sun rose higher and warmed the spring morning. Jesus sat in the shade of the great south wall. People milled about. They came and went. Some stayed for a few minutes. Others listened for hours. The disciples sat nearby or sometimes stood among the crowd. The chief priests, scribes, and elders were there watching too. They listened from the side, just inside Jesus' peripheral vision. Often Jesus spoke in parables. He told stories he had told many times before in Galilee. This day he had a new audience.

One story Jesus told was this:

"A man planted a vineyard, put a fence around it, dug a pit for the wine press, and built a watchtower; then he leased it to ten-ants and went to another country."† Jesus was relaxed. He enjoyed telling this tale. It was just a simple, curious story. Those listening, including the Temple leaders, fell into the parable.

"When the season came," Jesus said after a pause, "he sent a slave to the tenants to collect from them his share of the produce of the vineyard."† Still, it was just a simple story. But then Jesus leaned forward, put his hands on his knees, and spoke more quietly. His listeners strained forward to hear him. "But they seized him," Jesus said, laying each word out distinctly, "and beat him, and sent him away empty-handed."†

Jesus looked into blank faces. They looked back. He went on. "And again he sent another slave to them; this one they beat over the head and insulted. Then he sent another, and that one they"— he hesitated—"killed."† When the word "killed" slipped from his mouth, a lot of people gasped.

"And so it was," Jesus continued as he picked up his volume, "with many others; some they beat, and others"—he hesitated again—"they killed."†

The story was no longer a simple, curious tale. Jesus drew everybody into his razor-sharp parable. "He had still one other, a beloved son. Finally he sent him to them, saying, 'They will respect my son.'"† Some in the crowd looked at their neighbors and nodded or whispered, "Yes. Yes." Jesus continued, "But those tenants said to one another, 'This is the heir; come, let us kill him, and the inheritance will be ours.'"†

Jesus rolled through the rest of the story at a clip: "So they seized him, killed him, and threw him out of the vineyard. What then will the owner of the vineyard do?"† He hardly took a breath before his stern, measured voice answered his own question: "He will come and destroy the tenants and give the vineyard to others."†

Wild pigeons pecked at the feet of people in the Temple court-yard. Hands fidgeted. Nobody whispered. The silence was loud.

"Have you not read this scripture?"† Jesus quoted from Psalm 118: "The stone that the builders rejected has become the corner-stone; this was the Lord's doing, and it is amazing in our eyes."† Only then did Jesus sit back—his hands in his lap again, his lips cracked just a little, and smile creases pulling gently at the outside of his eyes.

The chief priests, scribes, and elders were wide-eyed. Their leader, though, leveled his eyes and shot a venomous gaze across the crowd at Jesus. He—all of them—had had enough. This parable was about them. They retreated in humiliation. As they went, there was talk among them of arresting Jesus right away. Most agreed. The leader, however, said, "No, not now," because he knew the crowd could turn against them.

These angry Temple leaders sent some Pharisees and Herodians to hear Jesus for themselves. They came to where he was teaching. The crowd opened to let them by because these were holy and important people.

One, a very tall man, stood in front of Jesus. He ran his hand through his beard and then brought both hands together in front of the bright, golden robe that fell from his shoulders. He looked down on Jesus in his coarse, brown, one-piece robe and said to him sweetly and slowly, "Teacher, we know that you are sincere, and show deference to no one; for you do not regard people with partiality, but teach the way of God in accordance with truth."† He looked around as he hesitated, and then, with his head tilted in mock deference, he asked Jesus, "Is it lawful to pay taxes to the emperor, or not? Should we pay them, or should we not?"† The Pharisee fought back a smirk. His colleagues cackled.

Jesus' face brightened. "Hum," he said. Jesus knew they were hypocrites by their sneers as much as their question. He stroked his own beard. A moment passed. Two. Then Jesus stood up. With hands on his hips, he looked straight at the Pharisee's darting black eyes and asked, "Why are you aggravating me?" No answer.

Another moment slid by. Jesus held out his left hand, palm up, fingers flicking back and forth. "Let me have a denarius. Let me see it. Give me one."

One of the Herodians who was with the Pharisees produced a denarius from a small goatskin pouch. He stepped forward and dropped it on Jesus' palm. Jesus brought the coin toward his chest. He looked at one side and then deftly rolled it over single-handedly to study the other. Everybody watched. Another awkward moment of silence.

Satisfied, Jesus held the coin between his thumb and forefinger and asked the Herodians and Pharisees calmly, "This head and face—whose is it, and whose name is on it?" The man who had produced the coin answered snidely, "The emperor's."†

Jesus nodded. He was still for a few seconds before he spoke. "Give to the emperor the things that are the emperor's, and to God the things that are God's."† With that, Jesus suddenly flipped the denarius off his forefinger with his thumb, and it spun, arcing high through the air. The Herodian fumbled to catch it but missed. The denarius fell on the stones and rolled. The lead Pharisee slapped his sandal on top of it, and the coin's owner reached down and snatched it up.

The Pharisees and Herodians were amazed, frustrated, and ashamed. They retreated back across the Temple courtyard.

Later, at about three in the afternoon, a group of Sadducees, Jewish leaders who do not believe in the resurrection, wanted to test Jesus. They, too, had a trick question. "Teacher," their spokesman said, stepping forward, "Moses wrote for us that 'if a man's brother dies, leaving a wife but no child, the man shall marry the widow and raise up children for his brother.'"†

Looking to the other Sadducees for support, the questioner continued. "There were seven brothers; the first married and, when he died, left no children; and the second married her and died, leaving no children; and the third likewise; none of the seven left children. Last of all the woman herself died. In the resurrection whose wife will she be? For the seven had married her."† The Sadducee crossed his arms.

Jesus didn't hesitate. He bit back, "You're completely off. You don't know the scriptures, and you don't understand God!" He gave no time for a response. "Look, when men and women are resurrected from the dead, they don't marry. They're more like angels from heaven."

Jesus stopped. He let his words sink in. He scanned the crowd, watched his disciples, and studied the Sadducees. "And as for the dead being raised," he continued, "have you not read in the book of Moses, in the story about the bush, how God said to him, 'I am the God of Abraham, the God of Isaac, and the God of Jacob'? He is God not of the dead, but of the living."† Jesus stopped again. He waited in the echo of his words. Then, he said simply, "You're absolutely wrong." The Sadducees hung their heads and slithered away.

Immediately a scribe came forward. He had heard the exchange about resurrection between Jesus and the Sadducees. He was impressed. So the scribe asked a sincere question: "Which commandment is the first of all?"†

Jesus perked up and answered straight out, "The first is, 'Hear, O Israel: the Lord our God, the Lord is one; you shall love the Lord your God with all your heart, and with all your soul, and with all your mind, and with all your strength.' "† Every single person there nodded in agreement. "The second is this," he continued. " 'You shall love your neighbor as yourself.' There is no other commandment greater than these."†

The scribe liked what he had heard. "Your answer is correct. God is one and there is none besides God. Also, to love God completely, and to love your neighbor as you love yourself—burnt offerings and sacrifices aren't important at all compared to these."

The scribe smiled. Jesus smiled, too. While they were looking at each other, Jesus said to him directly, "You are not far from the kingdom of God."† From then on, nobody asked him any more sneaky questions.

But Jesus had more to say that afternoon. A short time later he asked the crowd, "How can the scribes say that the Messiah is the son of David?"† He went on, "David himself, by the Holy Spirit, declared, 'The Lord said to my Lord, "Sit at my right hand, until I put your enemies under your feet."' " David himself calls him Lord; so how can he be his son?"†

At least a hundred people were still around him. They loved what he was teaching. It was refreshing and challenging. Then Jesus stood up. He stretched. He was almost done for the day. Waving his arm slowly above the sea of heads, he said, "Beware of the scribes, who like to walk around in long robes, and to be greeted with respect in the marketplaces, and to have the best seats in the synagogues and places of honor at banquets!"† To finish he said in a big voice, "They take over widows' homes and say long prayers just to look pious. They'll really be condemned."

Jesus crossed the Temple to the Treasury. Many followed. A dozen or so people were there, some giving alms. Four or five very rich people each cascaded a handful of coins into the basin. Just as Jesus arrived, a poor, hunched-over widow dressed in a tattered, blue gown drifted silently to the alms table. She stood, fumbling with something in front of her. Her hands worked a knot loose from a patch of cloth. The woman's arthritic thumb and index finger slipped between the folds and found her two copper coins worth a penny. These she gently placed on the silver tray. They didn't even plink as she put them in.

Everyone with Jesus saw what he'd seen. He turned and said to those nearby, "Believe me, this widow gave more than everybody else who dropped something in the collection plate." Jesus looked at the rich people who had made their offerings. He swept his arm backward as if erasing them and said, "All of them, you see, have given from what they have left over; but this poor woman gave all she had to live on."

When the widow turned from the table, she walked near Jesus. She had no idea who he was. Jesus didn't say anything, but he reached out and touched her tattered robe as she passed by.

Chapter 13

J ESUS AND HIS followers left the Temple. When they were by the East Gate on their way out, one of the disciples—it was Thaddaeus—turned around and was completely awed by the grandeur and mass of the Temple and its buildings. He was walking next to Jesus and, without really thinking, he nudged Jesus and said, "Rabbi, look at those huge stones and magnificent buildings!" Jesus stopped and turned to look at them too. He put one arm across Thaddaeus's shoulder and pointed to the Temple Mount with his free hand. "Do you see these great buildings?"† Thaddaeus nodded. "Not one stone will be left here upon another; all will be thrown down."† Thaddaeus pulled back and saw how serious Jesus' face was.

Jesus led his friends to the Mount of Olives above Gethsemane. They walked into a small grove of trees. Jesus sat against one of the old, knurled trees and invited those with him to sit too. The Temple that impressed Thaddaeus so much rose above them to the west. Andrew—along with James, John, and Peter, who were right next to Jesus—then asked in a low, private voice, "Tell us, when will this be, and what will be the sign that all these things are about to be accomplished?"†

The late afternoon sun danced through the leaves so that a mottled light played on Jesus' face. His eyes were clear, but his forehead was furrowed. He pulled his hair behind his ears as he often did. No one could have imagined what Jesus would say, or, for that matter, that he would talk for so long without stopping. With his legs crossed, his hands clasped in his lap, and his shoulders back, Jesus began with an ominous warning: "Beware that no one leads you astray."† The cadence of his voice was measured. He chose his words carefully: "Many will come in my name and say, 'I am he!' and they will lead many astray. When you hear of wars and rumors of wars, do not be alarmed; this must take place, but the end is still to come. For nation will rise against nation, and kingdom against kingdom; there will be earthquakes in various places; there will be famines. This is but the beginning of the birth pangs."† Jesus studied his friends' faces one by one. They were listening with rapt attention.

"As for yourselves," he said, "beware; for they will hand you over to councils; and you will be beaten in synagogues; and you will stand before governors and kings because of me, as a testimony to them."† The sobriety of Jesus' voice washed over the hearts and minds of those with him that day. The disciples were spellbound.

Jesus continued: "And the good news must first be proclaimed to all nations. When they bring you to trial and hand you over, do not worry beforehand about what you are to say; but say whatever is given you at that time, for it is not you who speak, but the Holy Spirit."† He paused, letting this, too, sink in. The disciples looked one to another—some with worry, some with resignation.

"Brother will betray brother to death, and a father his child, and children will rise against parents and have them put to death; and you will be hated by all because of my name. But the one who endures to the end will be saved."† Still, nobody spoke. Philip shifted uneasily. Dogs were always around, and two wandered through the group, sniffing for food. A shepherd with a small flock from the market—his dog herding the sheep—passed by on the road. He was heading to a fold outside Jerusalem for the night. The sun edged toward the horizon.

"But when you see the desolating sacrilege set up where it ought not to be (let the reader understand), then those in Judea must flee to the mountains; the one on the housetop must not go down or enter the house to take anything away; the one in the field must not turn back to get a coat."† Jesus had never before spoken so specifically or with such foreboding. These weren't parables.

"Woe to those who are pregnant and to those who are nursing infants in those days! Pray that it may not be in winter. For in those days there will be suffering, such as has not been from the beginning of the creation that God created until now, no, and never will be."†

Jesus reached for the waterskin. He drank, holding the sun-warmed water in his mouth before swallowing. He leaned forward just a little and said, "And if the Lord had not cut short those days, no one would be saved; but for the sake of the elect, whom he chose, he has cut short those days. And if anyone says to you at that time, 'Look! Here is the Messiah!' or 'Look! There he is!'—do not believe it. False messiahs and false prophets will appear and produce signs and omens, to lead astray, if possible, the elect. But be alert; I have already told you everything."†

Jesus relaxed against the tree. It was as if he was watching pictures in his mind. He leaned forward again and spoke once more: "But in those days, after that suffering, the sun will be darkened, and the moon will not give its light, and the stars will be falling from heaven, and the powers in the heavens will be shaken. Then they will see 'the Son of Man coming in clouds' with great power and glory."† Jesus' voice lifted as he said these things. "Then he will send out the angels, and gather his elect from the four winds, from the ends of the earth to the ends of heaven."†

Where Jesus got these ideas, the disciples didn't know. They were in awe and secretly frightened. But Jesus wasn't finished. "From the fig tree learn its lesson: as soon as its branch becomes tender and puts forth its leaves, you know that summer is near. So also, when you see these things taking place, you know that he is near, at the very gates. Truly I tell you, this generation will not pass away until all these things have taken place."† He paused. His friends waited.

"Heaven and earth will pass away, but my words will not pass away. But about that day or hour no one knows, neither the angels in heaven, nor the Son, but only the Father."† And then, as he again scanned from one face to another, Jesus said slowly and in his most serious tone yet: "Beware, keep alert; for you do not know when the time will come. It is like a man going on a journey, when he leaves home and puts his slaves in charge, each with his work, and commands the doorkeeper to be on the watch. Therefore, keep awake—for you do not know when the master of the house will come, in the evening, or at midnight, or at cock-crow, or at dawn, or else he may find you asleep when he comes suddenly. And what I say to you I say to all: Keep awake."†

Chapter 14

I
N TWO DAYS the Passover and the festival of Unleavened Bread would begin. Those chief priests and scribes of the Temple were still furious at what Jesus had done—wrecking the Temple and teaching his radical ideas all week long. He frightened them. The crowds who followed him also frightened them. The priests and scribes worked on a plan to take Jesus into custody secretly and to kill him. That was the only way they could really get rid of the man. But doing it during the high holy days was a problem. One wise scribe cautioned the council, "Not during the festival, or there may be a riot among the people."†

Jesus and the men and women who had come with him all the way from Galilee were staying in Bethany. It was evening, and Jesus was at table in the house of Simon the leper. When a tall woman joined the group, she walked straight to Jesus. Under the crook of her right arm, she held a large, alabaster jar. Standing in front of Jesus, the woman broke the seal on the top of the jar. It was full of expensive nard. Without the slightest permission or hesitation, she raised the jar and carefully poured the nard onto Jesus' head. The woman put the jar on the floor. The scarf covering her head slipped off and onto her shoulders. Her hair was thick and lush. Her eyes melted into Jesus' eyes. Slowly the woman's strong fingers massaged the nard into Jesus' scalp and hair. She rubbed his forehead, behind his ears, and the nape of his neck. Jesus' chin fell to his chest. He closed his eyes. The woman rubbed the ointment in passionately and lovingly.

Instantly, a buzz vibrated among his friends. Some were angry. Judas whispered too loudly, "Why was the ointment wasted in this way?"† He looked around for agreement and then continued gruffly, "For this ointment could have been sold for more than three hundred denarii, and the money given to the poor."† Peter got up and stepped over to the woman's side. He chastised her. But she never stopped pulling her strong fingers through Jesus' hair.

"Let her alone."† Jesus spoke quietly—his head bowed, his eyes still closed. The woman stayed in front of Jesus. The aroma of the nard and her own scent mixed together, and it was wonderfully pleasant. "Why do you trouble her?"† he asked. "She has performed a good service for me."†

After nearly ten minutes, Jesus lifted his head slowly. His eyes opened to the room's brightness, and he squinted. Jesus reached his hands up to the woman's oiled hands and brought her fingers to his lips. He kissed her fingers and didn't let go. He held her hands affectionately. Their eyes kissed.

"You always have the poor with you," Jesus began, "and you can show kindness to them whenever you wish; but you will not always have me."† Jesus looked deep into the woman's tear-filled, love-filled eyes and pulled her to his side as he continued: "She has done what she could; she has anointed my body beforehand for its burial. Truly I tell you, wherever the good news is proclaimed in the whole world, what she has done will be told in remembrance of her."† He brought her fingers back to his lips and kissed them again softly.

Judas Iscariot, who was an apostle, was upset by all of this—really angry. At first he was going to say something. He didn't. He looked into his lap; his stomach was twisting and turning. His heart raced. Sweat beaded under his arms, and he jiggled his leg uncontrollably. Things were not meant to be this way. This woman's waste of expensive nard was all wrong. Judas quietly slipped past his companions. Maybe they thought he was going to relieve himself. He left Simon's house and stepped into the darkness. Judas, his hands pulling at his hair, twirled around three times. Then he stopped. He knew what he would do—what he had to do.

On the road to Jerusalem, Judas picked up his pace. A dust cloud followed him in the darkness. He came to the city, passed through the East Gate, and climbed the Temple Mount. He would see the chief priests. He would tell them where and when they could find Jesus alone.

Judas barged into the Inner Court. He announced to the priests that he would help them. They looked at one another in amazement at their good fortune. Judas had solved their problem of how to capture Jesus. They promised Judas money, but he spun around and left. His heart still pounded in his chest, and his breath was quick. From that moment on, Judas waited for the chance to turn Jesus over to the chief priests.

The festival of Unleavened Bread arrived. This is the holy day of Passover when the sacrificial lamb is killed. It was midmorning. The disciples responsible for organizing the Passover meal—James, son of Alphaeus, and Philip—approached Jesus and asked him, "Where do you want us to go and make the preparations for you to eat the Passover?"†

Jesus brought his hand to his chin and tugged on his beard. He told the two, "Go into the city, and a man carrying a jar of water will meet you; follow him, and wherever he enters, say to the owner of the house, 'The Teacher asks, Where is my guest room where I may eat the Passover with my disciples?'"† Jesus looked at them to be sure they understood. He finished by saying, "He will show you a large room upstairs, furnished and ready. Make preparations for us there."†

Philip and James left Bethany for the city and entered through the Fountain Gate. Once inside the wall, a man carrying a water jar approached them just as Jesus had said. They followed the man, found the house, and told the owner, "The Teacher asks, Where is the guest room where he may eat the Passover with his disciples?" After they saw the large room upstairs and were satisfied, they arranged for the sacrifice of an unblemished lamb and its roasting. They also bought bread and wine. All was ready.

In the evening, Jesus and the twelve who had been with him since the start of his ministry in Galilee walked from Bethany to Jerusalem before the sun set. Philip and James showed Jesus and the others to the house and the upstairs room where everything was set up. They reclined at table together. As always, the celebration began as a festive time, a happy occasion.

Much later, after most of the meal had been eaten, Jesus became quiet. At first nobody noticed. But then his somber mood spread. Jesus, lying comfortably with these good, close friends, said with no emotion at all, "Truly I tell you, one of you will betray me, one who is eating with me."† He scanned the twelve.

This comment upset everybody. One after another they said something like, "It's not me, is it?"

Soberly, Jesus replied to all of them together, "It is one of the twelve, one who is dipping bread into the bowl with me. For the Son of Man goes as it is written of him, but woe to that one by whom the Son of Man is betrayed! It would have been better for that one not to have been born."†

The mood in the room darkened even more. Everyone felt it. Nobody ate anything else. After a short time, Jesus reached to the middle of the table and took one last, untouched loaf of flat bread. He lifted it in front of them as if to bless it, but then he just stared at the bread. Everyone was silent. No one fidgeted. A moth flew into an open lamp flame. A cat curled on the corner of a cushion. The disciples watched Jesus, wondering what he would do next.

Jesus lifted the bread a bit higher and spoke: "Blessed be God, sovereign of the universe, who brings forth bread from the earth." Then he broke the loaf in half—one chunk in his left hand and one in his right. Some crumbs fell to the table. Jesus broke the bread some more and passed the pieces to his friends, saying, "Take; this is my body."† The disciples had eaten bread with Jesus many times before, but these words were new. Each one took a piece and ate it without saying a word. Jesus ate a piece of bread too.

After this, Jesus picked up a cup of wine that was within easy reach. He raised it up and blessed it just as he had done with the bread: "Blessed be God, sovereign of the universe, who brings forth wine from the earth." He drank from the cup and passed it to Peter, who was sitting next to him. As Peter drank, Jesus said to them all, "This is my blood of the covenant, which is poured out for many. Truly I tell you, I will never again drink of the fruit of the vine until that day when I drink it new in the kingdom of God."† Strange words. Everyone drank from the cup. Afterwards, Jesus led them all in singing the second part of the Hallel psalms. The meal ended.

After the psalm, Jesus and his companions descended the stairs and went into the street. The night was bright with the full moon. A couple of alley cats scrapped. Very few people were out.

Jesus led them toward the garden called Gethsemane. Along the way he stopped, turned to the disciples, and said calmly, "You will all become deserters; for it is written, 'I will strike the shepherd, and the sheep will be scattered.' But after I am raised up, I will go before you to Galilee."†

That announcement was disturbing. Peter pushed forward to Jesus' side. He always had something to say, and this time he protested: "Even if everyone else runs away, I won't!" But Jesus took hold of Peter's elbow and squeezed it. Even in the darkness Jesus' eyes pierced Peter as he corrected his friend, "Truly I tell you, this day, this very night, before the cock crows twice, you will deny me three times."†

Peter yanked his elbow out of Jesus' grip. Almost shouting in Jesus' face, he blurted, "Even though I must die with you, I will not deny you."† And standing there like a clump of trees in the nighttime, all the rest said similar things. They promised not to desert Jesus.

Jesus heard them but, without saying another thing, proceeded toward the garden. This all happened near the Water Gate, about halfway to Gethsemane. When they arrived at the garden, Jesus turned to them and said quietly, "Sit here while I pray."† Then, he touched the sleeves of Peter, James, and John, signaling them to follow. The others sat down in small groups to wait.

Jesus was agitated, uneasy. He spoke to the three in an unfamiliar, gloomy voice. "I'm miserable and feel like I'm dying. Stay here and stay awake." They nodded OK. Jesus walked farther into the darkness, out of their sight. He dropped to the ground on his knees—his hands gripping the hair on the back of his head. Then Jesus lay on his stomach—one side of his face in the grass, his eyes closed, his arms outstretched. As he grabbed clumps of grass, his fingernails raked the dirt. His fingers closed in grass-filled fists.

"Abba, Abba, Abba." Jesus prayed that it might be possible for this crisis to pass. "For you all things are possible,"† he said aloud. His breaths were quick and shallow. His heart pounded. He turned his face upward. "Take this cup, God. Take it from me. Oh, God, take it away. Take it away." He paused. His body relaxed a little. Slowly he came up on his elbows, and peered into the emptiness. "Yet, not what I want, but what you want."†

Jesus pushed against the ground with still-clenched fists as he pulled his knees up under his chest. Then he stood up in the darkness—hands at his sides, grass still in his fists. He opened his hands, and the grass clumps and dirt fell to the ground.

Jesus walked back to where Peter, James, and John were, only to find them curled up and asleep. Jesus nudged Peter with his toe. "Simon, are you asleep? Could you not keep awake one hour?"† Peter looked at the black silhouette of Jesus above him. Jesus said, "Keep awake and pray that you may not come into the time of trial; the spirit indeed is willing, but the flesh is weak."†

Jesus went back into the moonlit garden. He fell to his knees again and then dropped back onto his heels. Jesus prayed some more. "Abba, Abba, Abba." He breathed deeply. "For you all things are possible; remove this cup from me; yet, not what I want, but what you want."† He stayed there for a long time—not thinking, just breathing, trying to settle his unquiet heart.

When Jesus returned to Peter, James, and John, he found them asleep again. They were exhausted and had had a bit too much to drink at the seder meal. They were at a loss for words when he nudged them awake a second time. And when he came back a third time and found them sleeping again, Jesus called, "Are you still sleeping and taking your rest? Enough! The hour has come; the Son of Man is betrayed into the hands of sinners. Get up, let us be going. See, my betrayer is at hand."†

While Jesus was speaking, Judas stepped into the garden. A crowd followed him. They had torches, swords, and clubs. The chief priests, the scribes, and the elders had sent this band to find Jesus. Jesus saw them approaching and calmly walked to meet them on the garden path. Peter, James, and John hopped up and dashed after Jesus. The other disciples jumped up too.

Now Judas, who had slipped away from the garden, told the leader of the crowd, "The one I will kiss is the man; arrest him and lead him away under guard."†

Judas and the rabble confronted Jesus. The disciple stared closemouthed at his teacher and friend. He looked back over his shoulder for the armed men. Jesus stood quietly and waited. Judas took three long strides, put his hands on Jesus' shoulders, and said, "Rabbi!"† and kissed him on the cheek.

Two armed men from the crowd immediately rushed forward and grabbed Jesus. One of the disciples had a sword. He drew it quickly and immediately hit the slave of the high priest on the side of his head. Blood splashed everywhere. The man screamed and held his robe to the bloody mess. His right ear had been sliced off.

Jesus, calm as could be, said to those holding him, "Have you come out with swords and clubs to arrest me as though I were a bandit? Day after day I was with you in the temple teaching, and you did not arrest me. But let the scriptures be fulfilled."† With that, the guards turned with Jesus in tow and marched back toward Jerusalem.

Right then the disciples deserted Jesus. They scattered. They feared because they were really scared of getting arrested too.

Now, there was a young man who had followed Jesus that night. He had on only a light linen cloth. Somebody in the crowd snatched at him to take him away with Jesus, but all he could grab was the linen cloth. The young man pulled back, and the gown slipped off—right over his head. He ran away stark naked.

Jesus was taken through the Water Gate to the courtyard of Caiaphas, the high priest. It wasn't far—only about three-quarters of a mile. There, the chief priests, the elders, and the scribes waited.

Now Peter ran along after Jesus, but not too close. And when he had the chance, he sneaked in with some others to see what was happening to Jesus. He hid amid the crowd and guards gathered around a fire that had been started.

The trial started. The chief priests and every member of the ruling council wanted people to testify against Jesus. They wanted evidence so they could have him executed, but there was none. A lot of people testified falsely against Jesus, and their testimony didn't agree with that of the others. One witness who stood up to speak said, "We heard him say, 'I will destroy this temple that is made with hands, and in three days I will build another, not made with hands.'"† But their stories were contrary to one another, and so the evidence was no good.

Then, it was Caiaphas's turn. He stood up in his rich and beautiful robes. His face was stern. He squinted, trying to see Jesus clearly in the torchlight. He asked Jesus, "What do you have to say for yourself? Why are all these people accusing you?"

Jesus was silent.

Again the high priest questioned Jesus, "Are you the Messiah, the Son of the Blessed One?"† This time Jesus spoke directly, "I am; and 'you will see the Son of Man seated at the right hand of the Power,' and 'coming with the clouds of heaven.'"†

Caiaphas's body shook. His face contorted. He raised his hands to the neck of his fancy robe and grabbed the collar. Suddenly he pulled down and ripped the robe apart. It was quite a display. Then Caiaphas shouted, "Why do we still need witnesses? You have heard his blasphemy! What is your decision?"† All of the priests and scribes of the council, and some people in the crowd, condemned Jesus. They said he deserved to die.

A few of the people near Jesus spat on him. One man tied a rag around Jesus' eyes. Others hit him and said, "Prophesy!"† Then, the guards grabbed him and dragged him over to the wall where they punched, kicked, and beat him. Some people cheered.

Meanwhile, Peter, still hiding out in the courtyard, watched what was happening to Jesus. One of Caiaphas's servant girls walked by and saw Peter beside the fire. The girl looked him over for a second or two and then said, "You also were with Jesus, the man from Nazareth."† She had seen him with Jesus when he was teaching in the Temple. Peter fidgeted. He turned his face away and said gruffly, "I do not know or understand what you are talking about."† Then he got up and went to the front of the court-yard. Suddenly, a cock crowed.

The servant girl circled around and, on seeing him more clearly, said to everybody nearby, "This man is one of them."† But again Peter twisted away and denied it. Not long after this, a man in the crowd said right to Peter's face, "Certainly you are one of them; for you are a Galilean."†

Irate, Peter's face turned crimson. People stepped back, afraid of what he might do. He swore aloud, "I do not know this man you are talking about."† And right then, a second cock crow was heard. The sound thundered at the bottom of Peter's soul. Then the words Jesus had said earlier came back to him: "Before the cock crows twice, you will deny me three times."† Peter's head dropped and his stomach wrenched. He wrapped his arms around himself and cried in the middle of the crowd in the middle of the high priest's courtyard in the middle of the night.

Chapter 15

THE NIGHT SKY slowly brightened into dawn. Torches were extinguished. Few people remained. Just after sunrise, the chief priests held a consultation with the elders and scribes and all the council members. They knew what they would do. They needed the Romans to kill Jesus.

Jesus sat with his hands tied in front of him and his back to the courtyard wall. Two guards stood over him. He had been there all night. He was cold, stiff, and sore. His head throbbed. When the order came, a burly guard yanked Jesus to his feet. The chief priests and guards took him through the quiet Friday morning streets of Jerusalem to the Praetorium at the edge of the Temple Mount, where the governor was.

Dressed in a white robe with gold trim, Pontius Pilate, the Roman governor, swaggered to the governor's bench and sat. Fat white ankles showed below the brocade hem of his gown. Helmeted palace guards flanked him—their tall banners proclaiming SPQR (*Senatus Populusque Romanus,* or Senate and People of Rome).

The two Temple guards pushed and prodded the red-eyed Jesus forward. More than anything, Jesus' mouth was dust dry. Pilate glared at the Jewish captive, who was so much like thousands of others who had come before him. Pilate was brusque. "Are you the King of the Jews?"† Jesus didn't hesitate. "You say so."†

The usual gaggle of curiosity seekers, plus some stragglers who had been at the courtyard of Caiaphas during the night, milled around the periphery of the Praetorium. The chief priests stood in a neat row off to the side. When their turn to speak came, one after another leveled accusations at Jesus, including blasphemy. Once again, Pilate queried Jesus, "Have you no answer? See how many charges they bring against you."†

Jesus said nothing more. He stood there tight-lipped. His body ached and his wrists were raw from rope burns. He could do nothing. He looked straight ahead at the governor. Pilate was shocked.

During the festival of Unleavened Bread, Pilate would often free one of the Jewish prisoners—whomever the people called to be released. It so happened that a prisoner named Barabbas—a murderous rebel zealot—was one of the Roman prisoners, and all the crowd knew this. So, when Pilate asked who they wanted him to release, they said Barabbas.

Pilate bellowed to the crowd, "Do you want me to release for you the King of the Jews?"† With a sly smirk on his face, he quickly scanned the group. Then Pilate stared straight at the Temple elite. They were defiant. They shook their heads and replied, "No." Pilate realized the priests were jealous of Jesus, which was why they had brought Jesus to him. Meanwhile, two priests turned and incited the crowd in favor of Pilate releasing Barabbas, not Jesus.

Pilate put one ring-studded, pudgy finger on his chin pretending that he was thinking. In a sarcastic tone, he asked slowly, "Then what do you wish me to do with the man you call the King of the Jews?"†

With the priests encouraging them, the crowd called back, "Crucify him!"†

Suddenly Pilate's tone shifted. He became stern. "Why, what evil has he done?"† he asked. But the priests and some in the crowd kept shouting, "Crucify him!"†

Pilate didn't really care what happened to Jesus. But it never hurt to satisfy the people and keep the priests obliged to him. So, with a wave of his hand, Pilate signaled the release of Barabbas. Another wave of his hand ordered the guards to flog Jesus.

A brawny Roman soldier stepped behind Jesus. In one swift move he pulled Jesus' tunic over his head, and it bunched up over his tied wrists. The soldier drew a short, flat, six-tailed whip from his belt. One. Two. Three. Four. Jesus' knees, which were weak already, suddenly buckled. He fell. Another guard pulled him to his knees. Five. Six. Seven. Blood and bits of flesh flew, and the chief priests stepped back, out of range. The paving stones reddened. Pilate yawned and cleaned his fingernails with a sliver of wood. Eight. Nine. Ten. Eleven.

When he was satisfied, Pilate waved his hand again, and the soldier stopped. The flogging had lasted nearly ten minutes. Jesus slumped and fell on his side. With one final wave of his hand, Pilate ordered Jesus crucified. The governor stood. He gawked at Jesus lying naked in his own blood. Jesus looked up as Pilate turned with a flourish and swaggered away.

A Roman soldier pulled Jesus' robe down over his head and jerked him to his feet. The duty soldiers pushed and dragged Jesus to the courtyard of the Praetorium, Pilate's headquarters. There, the whole cohort came together to mock the Jewish prisoner. First they cut Jesus' hands free. Then they stripped him naked and wrapped a ratty, old, purple cloak around him. A young soldier, a boy of nineteen, twisted thorn branches into a crown. He gave it to the sergeant of the guard, who pushed it cruelly onto Jesus' head. The thorns punctured Jesus' scalp. Rivulets of blood ran down his forehead, face, and the back of his neck. The Romans stood in military rank and offered a stiff-armed salute to Jesus. "Hail, King of the Jews!"† they all shouted.

The morning air went from cool to warm. Jesus was hot. He was exhausted and weak and very thirsty. The soldiers continued their joking and torturous fun. They struck Jesus' head with sharp reeds dozens of times. They spat on him, and the spittle ran into his eyes, down his nose, across his lips, and onto his chest. As Jesus stood weak-kneed in the courtyard, the soldiers knelt down and feigned homage to the "King of the Jews."

When the cohort finished, the guards jerked the blood-soaked purple cloak off Jesus' shoulders. The rough cloth rasped across the raw welts. The young soldier dropped Jesus' own one-piece wool robe back over his head and pushed him out of Pilate's head-quarters to crucify him.

From the Praetorium to the killing ground was only about four hundred yards. Jesus could barely stand. The guards loaded the cross-timber on his shoulders. After only ten steps, he collapsed under its weight. He couldn't catch himself as he fell. His elbows hit the road first; then his face smashed onto the dirt. The beam knocked the side of his head, pivoted, and tore across his left leg.

Just then, Simon of Cyrene—the father of Alexander and Rufus—was passing by. He was coming in from the country. The guards grabbed him and made him carry the cross-timber for Jesus. Simon knew better than to resist. Together Jesus and Simon staggered through the Judgment Gate to Golgotha (which means the place of a skull). A few of the chief priests and scribes followed the Romans and their prisoner, along with some of the people who had waited outside the Praetorium while Jesus was being beaten.

A seasoned, somewhat kindly old centurion held a cup of wine mixed with myrrh to Jesus' lips. He'd done this a hundred times before. He knew it would dull the pain. Jesus smelled it and turned his head away. The soldier threw the brew on the ground.

Then the nineteen-year-old guard yanked Jesus' tunic up and over his head, tearing again at the dried blood on his back. Jesus was numb. He stood there naked, completely naked. Another soldier hit Jesus behind the knees with the shaft of his spear. Jesus dropped to the ground like stone. The guard rolled Jesus over with his foot. Jesus lay splayed on his back, and they pushed the rough crossbeam under his head and shoulders. He couldn't have resisted even if he had wanted to. His strength was spent. As he looked up, the blazing yellow sun made silhouettes of the executioners standing over him.

A sudden shock of blue-white light shot through Jesus' left arm to his brain and back to his wrist. Another smashing blow—more sound than feeling—drove the big nail the rest of the way into the wood. Jesus involuntarily twisted to the side—his right hand flailing. His tongue was so swollen, he couldn't even scream.

In an instant, that hand was grabbed and the back of it smashed to the cross-timber. A heavy, sandaled foot crunched his wrist. The blue-white light flashed. Two thwacks again this time. Surprisingly, very little blood flowed from the wounds. Jesus' knees flinched and rose uncontrollably to his chest. Ropes were tied around the crossbeam and Jesus' arms because the nails didn't always hold.

Four soldiers lifted the crossbeam, with Jesus nailed to it, and dropped it onto the upright timber that was buried deep in the hard ground. With the pieces joined, the guard slammed a nail through each ankle and into the sides of the upright timber. There was blue-white light again, but not as much as before.

Jesus' weight settled on the cross, which tilted slightly left and leaned forward. His feet were barely off the ground. The charge against Jesus, written on a board nailed to a flat stick, was lashed to the top of the cross. It read, "The King of the Jews."†

Jesus' chest and lungs crushed down on his diaphragm. To breathe, he had to pull himself up and suck in the air. Every breath became a prayer.

The Roman soldiers didn't watch Jesus. They knew what was happening. It would take a while for him to die. While they waited, they took his clothes and rolled dice to see who got what. By the time Jesus was crucified, it was nine o'clock in the morning.

After Jesus was nailed to his cross, the Roman cohort crucified two notorious bandits. One was on Jesus' right and the other on his left. It was another day of killing.

As people came along, some made fun of Jesus. A particularly loud-mouthed man, who stood looking at Jesus, shook his head and said, "Aha! You who would destroy the temple and build it in three days, save yourself, and come down from the cross!"† The chief priests and scribes made fun of Jesus too. More than once they said snidely, "He saved others; he cannot save himself. Let the Messiah, the King of Israel, come down from the cross now, so that we may see and believe."† They got what they wanted: Jesus on the cross. The two bandits who were crucified with Jesus also taunted him.

At noon, the whole land suddenly became dark. This was odd, and the darkness lasted until three in the afternoon. It was then that Jesus shouted as loudly as he could, "Eloi, Eloi, lema sabachthani?" which means, "My God, my God, why have you forsaken me?"† He was reciting the Twenty-second Psalm. A bystander didn't understand and said to those next to him,

"Listen, he is calling for Elijah."† Another person ran back through the Judgment Gate and soon returned with a sponge soaked with sour wine. He put the sponge on a stick and held it to Jesus' mouth for him to drink. The man said, "Wait, let us see whether Elijah will come to take him down."†

Jesus, his body bloody and limp, could no longer lift himself to breathe. One last prayer-breath escaped his cracked and bloody lips. And at that moment, the Temple curtain tore right in half. Flies buzzed. A dog sniffed Jesus' feet. People stared.

Now a certain centurion who was on guard at Golgotha stood facing the cross and saw Jesus take his last breath. The centurion was moved. He surprised even himself when he said, "Truly this man was God's Son!"†

Not all of Jesus' followers had abandoned him. Some of the women had followed Jesus after he was betrayed and had witnessed the crucifixion from afar. Among them, of course, was Mary Magdalene, but also Mary the mother of James the younger and of Joses, and Salome. These faithful ones, and many others, had journeyed from Galilee to Jerusalem with Jesus, providing for Jesus and all the disciples for many months.

Jesus was crucified on the afternoon before the sabbath, when observant Jews were prohibited from working. So, when sunset was approaching, Joseph of Arimathea, who was a well-respected member of the council and who was seeking the kingdom of God, took a bold chance. He asked Pilate for Jesus' body. Pilate did not know if Jesus was dead or alive, so he called for a centurion and asked him. The centurion told Pilate that Jesus was dead. So, Pilate gave the body to Joseph. What difference was it to him? Besides, he was in a good mood that afternoon.

First, Joseph purchased some linen. Then he went to Golgotha where three dead Jews hung on three crooked crosses. Usually the Romans left the crucified to rot as an example to the people. Often dogs ripped at their feet and legs, birds pecked at their eyes, and people threw stones. Joseph spared Jesus that fate.

Mary Magdalene and Mary, Joses' mother, still kept watch. They saw Joseph return. He pulled Jesus' feet free from the cross. Then he lifted the crossbeam, and Jesus' dead weight toppled to the ground. He kneeled to release Jesus' arms. Joseph hoisted Jesus across his shoulder. He stood up under the weight of Jesus' limp body and carried him to a nearby tomb cut right into the rock. Joseph laid Jesus on the ground in front of the tomb. He unfolded the linen cloth and spread it across the flat shelf of the tomb—a large portion falling over the front edge. Joseph leaned down and slipped his arms under Jesus' shoulders and legs. He stood again and placed the body onto the linen cloth. Then he folded Jesus' hands across his chest and wrapped the extra cloth tightly over Jesus' body, tucking it snugly under his back.

The day was spent. Joseph was spent. He kissed Jesus' forehead and then stood back. A moment later he rolled a large, heavy sealing stone against the opening. It was done. Joseph touched the stone and slowly walked away.

In the growing darkness, the ever-faithful Mary Magdalene and the other Mary watched Joseph lay Jesus' body in the tomb. There was nothing more to do. The women returned to Bethany as the moon rose over the eastern horizon.

Chapter 16

WHEN THE SABBATH ended, just at dawn on Sunday, Mary Magdalene, Mary the mother of James, and Salome went back through Jerusalem, past the stinking Golgotha—the two bandits were still hanging on their crosses—to the tomb where Jesus' body had been laid on Friday evening. Mary Magdalene had spices with her to anoint her Jesus. She also carried a five-petal red rose.

As they walked in the soft dawn light, Mary Magdalene—her thick, lush, red hair framing the beauty of her sad, sad face—wondered out loud to the others, "Who will roll away the stone for us from the entrance to the tomb?"† But when they arrived at the place, they were astonished. The huge sealing stone had been moved away from the tomb. A sinking feeling hit the pit of Mary's stomach. Her Jesus was gone! She was stunned. But then a sudden leap in her gut woke her up and brought her back to life.

When the three women got closer to the tomb, they noticed a young man wearing a white robe sitting on the right side of the burial chamber. Now they were really shocked. Mary Magdalene grabbed Salome who was already holding onto Mary, James's mother.

The man simply said to them, "Do not be alarmed."† His voice was self-assured and pleasant. "You are looking for Jesus of Nazareth, who was crucified."† Mary Magdalene nodded. "He has been raised; he is not here. Look, there is the place they laid him,"† the man said as he patted the stone slab where he was sitting. The women gasped. The body of Jesus certainly wasn't there. The young man continued, "But go, tell his disciples and Peter that he is going ahead of you to Galilee; there you will see him, just as he told you."†

Mary Magdalene, the other Mary, and Salome still clutched one another. They trembled. Their palms were sweaty. They looked at one another, puzzled. Slowly the three backed away from the tomb. Then, they let go of one another and quickly fled. They ran back toward the city—Mary still gripping her sack of spices and the red rose. Because they were so terrified and amazed, they did not say a thing to anybody. They were afraid.

Study Guide

THROUGH MARK'S EYES invites you into the Jesus story—to walk the dusty roads, row in the boats on the Sea of Galilee, witness healings, stand in the Temple, and weep at the cross. This study guide, likewise, invites you to imagine yourself as one of Jesus' friends and followers two thousand years ago as you explore your own thoughts, feelings, and experiences about what is happening as the days and weeks of your travels together unfold. One challenge may be to release your twenty-first-century point of view as you imagine yourself living and ministering with Jesus.

This Study Guide is also designed to help you think about people and places, situations and circumstances, problems and solutions we all face in today's modern world. The overarching question, both as you imagine and as you consider your life in the present, is *What do I think about this?*

To begin, each participant in the group should read chapter 1, or the next assigned chapter, before the group meets. Groups of eight to twelve are often best for stimulating discussion. It is also recommended that you read the preface, as it explains how and why the book was written. Referring to the map in the front of the book, which shows where certain events occurred, will be particularly helpful as you have your discussions.

While a single teacher or group facilitator could lead every meeting, it can also be beneficial for different members of the group to convene and oversee each discussion session. The leader should be familiar with the text and questions in advance. Quite simply, the questions are intended to stimulate conversation. Do not feel that you must discuss them all, although sometimes you may find that worthwhile. The leader may want to make up new questions or solicit questions from participants. In addition, there may be times when it is instructive to read aloud sections of the text associated with certain questions.

Chapter 1

Jesus' Baptism

1. It may seem odd that Jesus chooses to be baptized. Why do you think Jesus does this? What might Jesus expect from baptism by John?

2. How might Jesus' baptism have influenced his life and ministry?

3. Baptism is the sacrament by which God adopts us. What does it mean to live with the awareness that God is always present to us? If you have been baptized, what does your baptism mean to you? If you have not been baptized, what are some of your thoughts and feelings about baptism?

Follow Me

4. Why do you think Peter, Andrew, James, and John drop everything to take up a new life with Jesus?

5. Zebedee is left alone in the boat. What do you think he may be thinking about his sons leaving with Jesus? What might others think as they see their relatives or friends taking up with Jesus?

6. What does it mean for you to follow Jesus today? What do you need to give up and what do you gain?

Jesus Heals Many People

7. As you have traveled with Jesus, you have seen him heal many people. What are some of the common characteristics of Jesus' healing techniques? For example, how does he use touch?

8. When the leper and Jesus first come together, what do you suppose each of them sees in the other? Who is Jesus to the leper? Who is the leper to Jesus? Be specific.

9. People get out of the way when the leper walks by, but Jesus touches the leper. Besides healing the leper, what else does Jesus teach through this healing?

10. Sometimes we can be afraid of people who have handicaps, deformities, or illnesses. Where do you see people like this in your everyday world? How do you tend to view people who are different from you? Why do you think you might be uncomfortable with people unlike you?

Chapter 2

A Man through the Roof

1. Some people are desperate for Jesus' healing. If you were one of the four brothers, how would you justify ripping a hole in the roof?

2. How would you compare Jesus' reaction to seeing the man come through the ceiling to Peter's reaction? If you were there, how would you react and why?

3. Jesus forgives the man, and the scribes call it blasphemy. Why do the scribes say, "It is blasphemy"?† How and why do you

think the scribes are threatened because Jesus breaks the accepted rules about forgiveness?

4. Jesus challenges the traditional Jewish rules about forgiveness. When might it be necessary to challenge rules today, and why?

Eating Together

5. Unlike the scribes and Pharisees, Jesus practices open commensality—that is, he eats with everybody, even the unsavory, unclean, outcasts, and riffraff. What do you think about this practice? What are you saying when you welcome *all* to the table?

6. If you have ever been discriminated against, what did it feel like? If you have ever witnessed discrimination, tell what happened. What did you do to intervene?

7. Jesus says, "Those who are well have no need of a physician, but those who are sick."† What do you think Jesus means? Who is he talking about?

The Pharisee's Rules

8. The Pharisee criticizes Jesus because Jesus doesn't follow Jewish law. Why do you think Jesus so often goes against the established customs and laws? What is his point?

9. Jesus is a Jew. Like most Jews of his time, Jesus knows the Hebrew scripture very well. How does he use this knowledge to turn Jewish law and conventional wisdom upside down?

10. How might you feel if you were the Pharisee?

Chapter 3

Healing in the Synagogue

1. Sometimes it seems that Jesus does things just to provoke the

authorities. Explain why you think he heals the man with the deformed hand on the sabbath.

2. Why do the Pharisees want to get rid of Jesus?

Calling the Twelve

3. Jesus has many disciples. Why do you think he selects twelve to be apostles?

4. What does Jesus expect of his apostles? Be specific. By comparison, are Christians today expected to do the same? How are modern followers of Jesus supposed to live?

Jesus and His Family

5. Some of the people who see Jesus' healings think he is possessed by evil spirits. How does Jesus face the accusation that the devil helps him cast out demons?

6. Jesus says, "If a kingdom is divided against itself, that kingdom cannot stand. And if a house is divided against itself, that house will not be able to stand."† How does this argument serve Jesus' purpose in rebutting the scribes? How do people use the argument and this quote from scripture today? Give specific examples.

7. Jesus embarrasses his mother, brothers, and sisters, so they come to get him. Yet who does Jesus say is his family? What is his point? Explain.

Chapter 4

Parable of the Sower

1. Jesus is a masterful teacher. He often uses parables. How would you explain what a parable is?

2. How and why do parables enhance Jesus' teaching?

3. Jesus tells the parable of the sower. What do you think he means afterward when he says, "Let anyone with ears to hear listen!"†?

4. Which example of seed falling to the ground is most like you and why?

5. Jesus says God's domain is like a mustard seed. Why do you think he uses this example?

A Storm on the Sea of Galilee

6. Crossing the Sea of Galilee in an open boat is dangerous. As you imagine yourself with Jesus in a small boat in the middle of a storm, how do you feel? Explain what your real fear is.

7. When Jesus wakes up, what would you say to him?

8. What do you think is the significance of Jesus calming the storm?

9. Do you think Jesus inspires or frightens his disciples by calming the storm? Explain your answer.

Chapter 5

The Demoniac at Gerasene

1. Imagine that you are with Jesus and you see a madman running toward him. What do you do?

2. Perhaps you've noticed that demons always recognize Jesus. Why do you think this happens?

3. The demoniac is possessed by many demons. How does modern medicine diagnose people like this? What happens in our world today to people like the demoniac?

4. In Jesus' day and today, pigs are profane to the Jewish people. Why did Jesus send the demons into the pigs?

5. Jesus cures the demoniac, but he doesn't let him come with him. Why not? How would you feel if Jesus left you behind?

Jarius's Daughter and the Bleeding Woman

6. Conventional wisdom and Jewish law say that if somebody impure touches a clean person, the clean person becomes dirty. What happens when the bleeding woman, thought to be unclean, touches Jesus?

7. In Mark's Gospel, every person near to death whom Jesus encounters comes back to life. What do you think is the purpose or significance of this?

8. Jesus tells Jarius, and Jarius's wife and daughter, not to tell anybody about this healing. Why do you think he wants to keep it a secret? Explain whether or not you would be able to keep the secret and why.

Chapter 6

Jesus at Home in Nazareth

1. Although Jesus brings a new wisdom to his commentary on Torah, why do you think some of the people turn against him?

2. What do you think Jesus means when he says, "Prophets are not without honor, except in their hometown"?† How is Jesus a prophet?

3. Imagine yourself leaving the synagogue with Jesus. What do you say to him?

The Story of John's Death

4. Mark tells the story of John the Baptizer's death in great detail. Why do you suppose it was so important to Mark to include this story in the Gospel?

5. Herod makes a regrettable promise to his stepdaughter. Have you ever said something you wished you could take back? What did you say? What happened?

The Twelve Go Out Two by Two

6. Imagine going around the countryside healing the sick and talking about the *good news*. What do you think that would have been like in Jesus' time, and how would it be different today?

7. Why do you think Jesus sends the twelve out without him in groups of two?

Feeding the Five Thousand

8. Five loaves and two dried fish feed more than five thousand people. Imagine yourself among the crowd. What do you think about this miracle? What do you think of Jesus?

9. Given the stratification of society in Jesus' day, what other kind of miracle—besides providing enough food—does Jesus accomplish that day?

10. How does this event anticipate the Eucharist?

Walking on Water

11. For some observers, Jesus' miracles are contrary to the natural world—such as walking on the Sea of Galilee. Discuss how the miracles reveal that Jesus interacts with nature on an uncommon plane.

12. How do the miracles influence the way Jesus' contemporaries look at him, and why?

13. How are Jesus' miracles important to your understanding of who Jesus is?

Chapter 7

Jesus Challenges the Purity Laws

1. The Pharisees and scribes keep attacking Jesus. What do you know about them? What has Jesus done to make them so angry?

2. In Jesus' day, being ritually pure means you are acceptable to God. How do you think Jesus views this idea? What do you think he wants to change and why?

3. Jesus says that what goes in the body doesn't defile, but what comes out can defile. What do you think Jesus is talking about, and do you agree with him? Give two examples from our own time to illustrate your answer.

Jesus Is Taught a Lesson

4. Jesus is dismissive of the Syrophoenician woman. What does she teach him?

5. How might Jesus change because of this encounter? Explain.

6. What did you learn from this story? Be specific.

A Deaf Man Is Healed

7. When Jesus heals the deaf man, he says, " 'Ephphatha,' that is, 'Be opened.' "† How might this healing also be understood as a metaphor? Explain what it means to be open and why this matters.

8. Jesus puts his fingers in the deaf man's ears and also touches his tongue. If you were the deaf man, how might you react to what Jesus does?

9. As he often does, Jesus warns the man not to tell anybody about the healing. Why do you think he does this?

Chapter 8

Feeding the Four Thousand, Signs, and Yeast

1. In chapter 8, we have another feeding miracle. Why do you think Mark (and only Mark among the Gospels) includes two stories that are so much alike?

2. How do the two stories differ?

3. People want Jesus to show them signs from heaven. Why are signs so important to some people? Do signs matter to you? Why or why not?

4. What is the purpose of yeast in baking bread? Why does Jesus use yeast as a teaching metaphor?

5. What do you think Jesus wants the twelve to understand about "the yeast of the Pharisees"†?

A Blind Man Is Healed

6. The blind man literally receives his sight. How can you understand this healing as a metaphor? Explain what you mean and why it matters.

7. Tell of a moment when your eyes were suddenly opened and you saw something with fresh eyes.

You Are the Messiah

8. Jesus asks, "Who do people say that I am?"† What does it mean to be the Messiah? In other words, who is the Messiah meant to be and what is he meant to do for the Jewish people?

9. Why do you think Jesus insists that the disciples keep it secret that he is the Messiah?

10. What do you think of when you hear the phrase "Son of Man"? How is Jesus the Son of Man? How does this differ from Son of God?

11. Jesus rebukes Peter by saying, "Get behind me, Satan!"† How do you think Peter represents Satan here? Be specific.

12. Jesus says, "For those who want to save their life will lose it, and those who lose their life for my sake, and for the sake of the gospel, will save it."† This is an oxymoron. What do you think Jesus means, and why does he use an oxymoron to teach this idea?

Chapter 9

The Transfiguration

1. Jesus appears with Elijah and Moses. What does it mean that James, John, and Peter see Elijah and Moses with Jesus?

2. This is the second time in Mark's Gospel that we hear Jesus proclaimed "my Son." The first time was just after Jesus' baptism. Discuss how these events are similar and different.

3. What do you think happens to Jesus on the mountain? How is he changed by the transfiguration?

4. Once again, Jesus tells his friends to keep what they have witnessed a secret. Would you be able to keep this secret? If you didn't keep it, what would you say happened on the mountaintop?

Jesus Heals the Boy with Epilepsy

5. In Jesus' day, "spirits," not medical conditions, were believed to cause sickness. Discuss how both medical science and prayer are used today for healing the sick.

6. What do you think Jesus means when he says, "All things can be done for the one who believes"?

Troubling and Difficult Ideas

7. The first will be last and the last will be first is a strange notion. What is Jesus trying to teach his disciples? How does this apply to you?

8. Jesus talks about cutting off hands and feet if they become a stumbling block. He doesn't mean it literally, so why do you think he uses this language? What is his point?

9. What do you think Jesus is talking about when he says, "Have salt in yourselves, and be at peace with one another"†? Are you "salted"? Explain.

Chapter 10

Jesus Heads toward Jerusalem

1. According to Jesus, one man plus one woman joined in marriage does not equal two, but one. How is this a good description of marriage?

2. Jesus' comments about divorce are contrary to Jewish law and custom. How might Jesus' thinking support greater equality between men and women?

Jesus and Children

3. How do you think Jesus' love for children, at a time when children were not valued as they are today, set an example for his followers about caring for others?

4. Jesus contends that the kingdom of God belongs to little children. Why do children matter to Jesus? What do you think Jesus is getting at when he says this?

The Rich Man

5. The rich man seems to have done everything right. What does Jesus say the man is lacking?

6. Some people are owned by their possessions. How do you think Jesus wants you to care for the greater good with your own abundance?

7. Can an individual both follow Jesus and accumulate great wealth? Explain your thinking.

8. A camel can't get through the eye of a needle. Explain why this metaphor is so effective in making Jesus' point.

First Are Last

9. Jesus has a radical idea of family. What is Jesus' idea of family? How can we today apply his concept to our own families and to others?

10. Who are the "last" and the "first" today? Explain your response.

Foreshadow of Death

11. Jesus predicts his death and resurrection. As you imagine yourself among the twelve, how does Jesus' prediction sound to you? How do you react? What do you say?

12. What lesson do you think James and John forget when they ask to sit next to Jesus in heaven?

13. Jesus turns things upside down when he talks about being a servant. Explain why you think this is so important to Jesus. How are you a servant?

Blind Bartimaeus

14. Bartimaeus has heard of Jesus. What do you think he expects of Jesus and why?

15. Why do the townspeople, who know Jesus' reputation, shout at Bartimaeus to be quiet and leave Jesus alone?

16. Jesus says to Bartimaeus, "Go; your faith has made you well."† Do you think this means that Bartimaeus's faith alone heals him? Or, do you think Jesus does something to heal him? Explain what you mean.

Chapter 11

Jesus Enters Jerusalem

1. How might Jesus' entry into Jerusalem threaten the Romans?

2. "Blessed is the one who comes in the name of the Lord"† are the same words found in Psalm 118:26. How do you think Jesus' entry into Jerusalem recapitulates parts of Psalm 118?

3. Why do you think so many people parade with Jesus, and what might they expect from him?

Jesus Causes Big Trouble

   4. What does Jesus find when he enters the Temple, and why does it make him so angry?

   5. Why do you think Jesus' outburst threatens the Temple leaders?

   6. As you imagine yourself in the Temple that day, how would you react to Jesus? As a disciple? As a bystander? As one of the Temple elite?

The Fig Tree

   7. It seems very strange that Jesus would curse a fig tree and cause it to wither. Why do you think Mark includes this event? What does it teach?

   8. Why do you think Jesus says forgiveness is key to staying in touch with God?

Jesus and the Temple Elite

   9. It sometimes seems that Jesus is intentionally trying to aggravate the Temple elite. Do you agree? Why or why not?

  10. Jesus does not answer the Temple elite. What does this say about Jesus' attitude toward those who taunt him?

Chapter 12

Jesus Teaches in the Temple

   1. Jesus' parable about the vineyard owner attacks the chief priests, scribes, and elders. What is Jesus saying about them and what they do or do not do?

   2. Mark foreshadows Jesus' crucifixion with this parable. What does it also say about the role of the Temple elite in the death of Jesus?

Render to Caesar

   3. The Jewish people hate paying taxes to the Romans. Jesus uses

this situation to teach an important lesson. What do you think he is teaching regarding taxes?

4. Caesar claims to be the "son of god." Jesus says, "Give to the emperor the things that are the emperor's, and to God the things that are God's."† How does his statement challenge both the Romans and the Pharisees and Herodians? Explain.

Jesus Teaches All Afternoon

5. In Jesus' day there is a great debate among the Jewish people about resurrection. What does Jesus think about resurrection, and how does he prove his point?

6. Jesus tells the scribe that he's not far from the kingdom of God. Explain what you think Jesus means and why.

7. Jesus says the scribes are interested only in themselves. How do you think he wants the scribes to behave, and why does this matter?

Widow's Mite

8. What do you think of the widow who puts in two copper coins, "everything she had"†? Is she generous or foolish? Explain.

9. Giving to the church or other charities is often challenging. Should we give from what is left over or from the whole of our abundance? Explain. Is it important to tithe? Why or why not?

Chapter 13

Jesus Anticipates Hard Times Ahead

1. Jesus uses the Temple as a metaphor. Explain what he means.

2. Jesus paints a dark picture of things to come. Why do you think he does this? What purpose does this serve?

3. One might see this apocalyptic teaching as Jesus telling his disciples what they can expect. Why is it so important to

"keep awake," and what do you think Jesus means by that? Are you awake? Explain what you mean.

Chapter 14

Jesus Is Anointed; Judas Is Upset

1. An anonymous woman anoints Jesus with oil. Just as Jesus predicted, she is remembered today. Why? How is she the epitome of all that Jesus has been teaching?

2. Why is Judas upset about the expensive oil? Does he have good reason to be angry? Why or why not?

3. Besides "wasting" the oil, what makes Judas so disappointed with Jesus? What might he want Jesus to do?

The Last Supper

4. Jesus and his friends have eaten together scores of times. Yet this meal is different. How? Why is it so memorable? Be specific.

5. The bread and wine become a metaphor for Jesus' body and blood. They also reflect the ancient Jewish ritual of Passover. What is Passover, and how does it relate to Jesus at the Last Supper?

6. As you imagine yourself with Jesus on this night, what do you think about his words, "This is my body"† and "This is my blood"†?

Gethsemane Betrayal

7. The twelve, especially Peter, say they will stick by Jesus. But soon, Peter, James, and John begin to slip. How? What happens to their will? Why?

8. Jesus is distressed. Put yourself in his sandals. What does it feel like? What would you be thinking? What would your fears be? Would you want to escape?

9. Judas betrays Jesus with a kiss. Discuss the irony of Judas's kiss in light of the kiss of peace, which is shared in many Christian churches.

10. Judas is not the only one to betray Jesus that night. Discuss this idea.

11. Nobody knows who the young man is who runs away. Use your imagination and suggest who you think he is and what he is doing there.

Are You the Messiah?

12. When the high priest questions him, Jesus affirms that he is "the Messiah, the Son of the Blessed One"†. How do you think this seals his fate?

13. In the courtyard, Peter says, "I do not know this man you are talking about."† Why do you think Peter denies knowing Jesus? If you were in his shoes, what would you do? What might happen to you if you say you know Jesus?

Chapter 15

Pontius Pilate's Interview

1. If Jesus is "King of the Jews,"† how and why might that infuriate Pontius Pilate? What's the threat?

2. It's odd that the man released by Pilate is named Barabbas. *Bar* in Aramaic means "son," and *Abba* is the word Jesus uses when speaking of God. It is best translated "daddy." What do you make of the fact that the man Pilate releases is named Barabbas, or son of god?

3. The crowd says, "Crucify him!"† Who are those stirring up the crowd, and why do they want Jesus crucified so badly?

4. The flogging of Jesus seems so cruel. Can you imagine a positive side to the Romans' flogging of the condemned? Explain.

Hail, King of the Jews

5. Jesus is mocked with a crown of thorns. Why do you think the Romans do this, and what do you think they are trying to demonstrate to the Jews of Jerusalem?

6. Jesus tries to carry the cross-timber to Golgotha. How would you feel if you were Simon of Cyrene? Explain.

7. Imagine the shock of pain Jesus feels when the nails pierce his hands. What would you do to get through that experience? What would you pray in those moments?

8. Jesus is crucified with two bandits. What do you think ordinary people passing by think when they see these three men on crosses? How do you think that serves the Romans' purpose?

The End

9. Jesus says, "My God, my God, why have you forsaken me?"† This sounds so sad. Read all of Psalm 22, and discuss why you think Jesus speaks part of this Psalm as his last words. Or, explain why you think Jesus prays the psalm at the end.

10. A centurion standing nearby speaks out when Jesus dies. What does he say? When are two other times words like these are spoken in Mark's Gospel? What is the significance of hearing these words at the time of Jesus' death?

Joseph of Arimathea and the Women

11. The Jewish sabbath begins at sundown on Friday. Why do you think it is so important to Joseph that Jesus is buried before the sabbath starts?

12. Jesus' apostles desert him, but the women who are his disciples do not. What do you think about this? Why do you think they remain loyal and stay with Jesus, even at the cross?

Chapter 16

Afraid

1. Mary Magdalene and her friends return to the tomb. Why do you think they do this? If you were one of the women with Jesus, why might you go to the tomb?

2. "He has been raised,"† says the young man dressed in white. What do you think it means that Jesus "has been raised"†?

3. Mary and the other women are afraid. Why? What would you be afraid of if you were one of them? Explain.

Concluding Questions

1. Explain how *Through Mark's Eyes* has connected you to the Jesus story.

2. Explain how reading *Through Mark's Eyes* might inspire you.

3. How might you change because of this experience?

Blessings and the Peace of Christ be with you now and always.

Acknowledgments

ALTHOUGH I PENNED the manuscript, the finished product is the result of the insight, advice, and editing of many people. From the outset, my wife, Joanne Kimball, provided constant support and encouragement. She always knew *Through Mark's Eyes* would be published and widely distributed. I give her continued heartfelt love and thanks for being at the center of my life.

Since the earliest days of the first draft, author Anne Batterson slipped me nuggets of wisdom about writing and editing. She and John Spalding tutored me in the world of publishing. Their gentle guidance is greatly appreciated.

My deepest thanks to the people of Old St. Andrew's Episcopal Church in Bloomfield, Connecticut, where I am privileged to serve as Rector. At the top of that list is Dan Watson, who has always "held the space" for me. Thanks, too, to Karen Antonucci, my able assistant, a good friend, and a masterful speller.

Many parishioners and friends—specifically, Alison Swayne, Isabel Smith, Barbara Bell, Shirley Greiman, Cynthia Holmes, John Russell Smith, David Ingram, Barby Howe, Carolyn and Ed Phillips, George Vondermuhll, Margi Atwood, Di Hughes, Sally Jett, Bunny Millan, Charlie and Judith Danzoll, and Phyllis Armstrong—read early versions of the book and shared their comments and constructive criticisms. Most especially, I am grateful for the sharp pencils of Lorraine Taylor and Gretchen LaBau, copy editors extraordinaire. Thanks, too, to Mark Swayne for creating the map and key of Galilee.

Special appreciation to friends and acquaintances who read the manuscript and offered their thoughts about the project's concept as well as the text itself—David Owen, John Shelby Spong, Frank Runyeon, Tony McCague, Roger Cox, Caroline Fairless, William Countryman, Wilfredo Ramos-Orench, and Dick Mansfield. Eternal thanks to my great teacher, mentor, and fellow sheep farmer, the late William H. Armstrong, for his friendship and wisdom. And I will always be grateful to Elaine Ault, my spiritual guide and friend for more than twenty-five years.

Through Mark's Eyes is inspired by the many scholars who have begun to deepen our understanding of the historical Jesus. These especially include John Dominic Crossan and Marcus Borg. In addition, actor Frank Runyeon's one-person show "Afraid: The Gospel of Mark" helped me get started and continues to stimulate my imagination.

I readily confess that it was the presence of Jesus that brought Mark's Gospel to life in me and which I offer back to you.